# HOW JESUS FULFILLED THE LAW

## A PRONOMIAN POCKET GUIDE TO MATTHEW 5:17-20

### DAVID WILBER

**How Jesus Fulfilled the Law: A Pronomian Pocket Guide to Matthew 5:17-20**

Copyright © 2024 David Wilber. All rights reserved.

Pronomian Publishing LLC
Chatsworth, GA 30705

ISBN: 979-8-9908630-0-2

Publisher grants permission to reference short quotations (fewer than 300 words) in reviews, magazines, newspapers, websites, or other publications. Request for permission to reproduce more than 300 words can be made at **www.pronomianpublishing.com/contact**

Unless noted, all scriptural quotations are from The Holy Bible, English Standard Version, copyright © 2001 by Crossway Bibles, a division of Good News Publishers. Used by permission. All rights reserved.

David makes a compelling case for the pronomian reading of Yeshua's teaching in Matthew 5:17-20. Messianic Jews and Bible-believing Christians will greatly benefit from this extremely well documented book. God's Torah turns out to be relevant to the life of a believer in the twenty-first century.
—**Dr. Igal German**, Bibleapologist.org & Yesodbiblecenter.com

David's treatment of Matthew 5:17-20 provides readers with an easy-to-understand and cogent defense of pronomianism. His interpretation offers a cohesive, coherent, and comprehensive case as to why antinomian theologies cannot remain consistent with Christ's words, nor with their own theological commitments. If you are interested in providing evidence for why you choose to obey the Torah or want to understand Pronomian Christianity or Messianic Judaism more thoroughly, this book is a good starting place.
—**Dr. Gregory Scott McKenzie**, ThePronomian.com

Wilber's exposition of Matthew 5:17-20 is a notable step in restoring the correct understanding of Yeshua's relationship with the Torah and in building up pronomian scholarship.
—**Dr. Benjamin Szumskyj**, Teacher and Author of *Souls Knit Together: Thirty-One Lessons on Friendship from David and Jonathan*

# ACKNOWLEDGEMENTS

This book would not have been possible without the unwavering support and love of my wife, Rebecca. Thank you for being amazing.

I am also deeply grateful to my colleagues, Dr. Igal German, Dr. Scott McKenzie, and Mark Jacob. Your insightful feedback and meticulous editing were invaluable in refining this work.

# CONTENTS

Introduction .................................................................... 1

1. What It Means to Fulfill the Law (Matthew 5:17) ....................... 5
2. Until Heaven and Earth Pass Away (Matthew 5:18) ................ 19
3. Do and Teach the Commandments (Matthew 5:19) ................ 27
4. Be Better Than the Scribes and Pharisees (Matthew 5:20) ......... 39

Conclusion .................................................................... 47

Appendix: Have Things Already Passed From the Law? ................ 51

Postscript ..................................................................... 75

Bibliography ................................................................. 77

# INTRODUCTION

Should Christians keep the Law of Moses (a.k.a. the "Torah")?[1] In the Second Century AD, a teacher named Marcion argued that they should not. He taught that Christians could not follow the Law of Moses and the Gospel of Jesus at the same time. Tertullian, an early Christian apologist, explains that Marcion's teachings focused on showing the supposed incompatibility between the Law and the Gospel: "The separation of Law and Gospel is the primary and principal exploit of Marcion" (*Adversus Marcionem* 1.19).[2] Marcion believed that the entire Old Testament was the word of a lesser deity and urged Christians to unhitch from it entirely.[3]

Although the early Christians condemned Marcion as a heretic,[4] some modern Christian teachers hold a view of the Law similar to Marcion's.[5] For instance, we hear echoes of Marcion's antinomian ("against-

---

[1] Throughout this book, I will use the terms "Law" and "Torah" interchangeably. I use these terms to refer to the "Law of Moses"—that is, the commands delivered to God's people through Moses in Exodus, Leviticus, Numbers, and Deuteronomy.

[2] Turtullian, *Adversus Marcionem*, ed. and transl. Ernest Evans (New York, NY: Cambridge University Press, 1972), 49.

[3] Justo L. González, *The Story of Christianity, Vol. 1: The Early Church to the Dawn of the Reformation* (New York, NY: HaperCollins, 2010), 74.

[4] Ibid., 73.

[5] To be clear, there are notable differences as well. For example, these modern teachers

law") teachings in the words of megachurch pastor Andy Stanley. In his book *Irresistible*, Stanley insists that the Law "has no say in the life of a believer. None."[6] According to Stanley, Christians shouldn't even obey the Ten Commandments: "The Ten Commandments have no authority over you. None. To be clear: Thou shalt not obey the Ten Commandments."[7]

Why does Stanley believe that the Torah shouldn't guide our behavior as Christians? Because according to him, Jesus's death on the cross "fulfilled" the Torah, which rendered it obsolete. As Stanley writes, "Jesus did not abolish the law when he fulfilled it. But in fulfilling it, he made it...obsolete."[8] Here, Stanley appeals to Matthew 5:17, where Jesus announces that he came to "fulfill" the Law and Prophets. Stanley understands this verse to mean that Jesus came to fulfill the Messianic prophecies found in the Law and Prophets by dying on the cross, thereby bringing the Law and Prophets to completion. More recently, Christian theologian R. L. Solberg has made this same argument. In his book *Torahism*, Solberg writes that Jesus's death "fulfilled what the Torah was pointing toward," and this means that "Christians today are not bound by the legal requirements of the Law of Moses."[9] Solberg argues that Jesus's work on the cross brought the Law of Moses

---

    do not claim that the Hebrew Scriptures are the Word of a lesser deity. However, like Marcion, they *do* think that the Law of Moses has no authority over Christian conduct.

6    Andy Stanley, *Irresistible: Reclaiming the New that Jesus Unleashed for the World* (Grand Rapids, MI: Zondervan, 2018), 136.

7    Ibid.

8    Ibid., 110.

9    R. L. Solberg, *Torahism: Are Christians Required to Keep the Law of Moses?* 2nd ed. (Franklin, TN: Williamson College Press, 2022), 157.

to an end: "The Mosaic Law was always intended to be temporary; its divine expiration date was the arrival of Jesus."[10]

Jesus *did* say that he came to fulfill the Law and Prophets in Matthew 5:17. But what did he mean by this? Are Andy Stanley and R. L. Solberg correct in teaching that Jesus brought the Law of Moses to an end through his work on the cross? Is *that* what Jesus meant when he said that he came to fulfill the Law? Did Marcion have a point about the need for Christians to set the Law aside?[11]

I don't think so. I contend that the approach taken by interpreters like Stanley and Solberg completely misses the point of Matthew 5:17-20. Jesus is *not* declaring that his work on the cross brings the Law to an end. Instead, as I will demonstrate in this short book, Jesus declares the opposite message: *the Law remains binding and authoritative.*

The following chapters of this book are structured around each verse in Matthew 5:17-20. I will present a pronomian ("pro-law") interpretation of each verse and a response to common antinomian objections. I will argue the following:

- Chapter 1: Jesus announces that he did not come to nullify the Law but instead came to teach his followers how to keep the Law properly (Matt. 5:17).
- Chapter 2: Jesus states that the whole Law will remain in effect as long as heaven and earth exist (Matt. 5:18).
- Chapter 3: Jesus urges his followers to obey and teach the commandments found in the Law of Moses (Matt. 5:19).

---

10   Ibid.
11   I am not the only person who sees similarities between Marcionism and Andy Stanley's statements about the Law. See R. Albert Mohler, "Getting 'Unhitched' from the Old Testament? Andy Stanley Aims at Heresy," *Albert Mohler*, Aug. 10, 2018.

- Chapter 4: Jesus requires his followers to be better than the scribes and Pharisees at keeping the Law (Matt. 5:20).

After thoroughly examining Matthew 5:17-20 in Chapters 1-4, I will conclude with a brief discussion of the theological implications of my interpretation. I have also included an appendix that will address some objections to my interpretation of Matthew 5:18 in greater depth.

I hope this short book blesses you and gives you a greater understanding of how Jesus fulfilled the Law.

# CHAPTER 1
# WHAT IT MEANS TO FULFILL THE LAW
## (MATTHEW 5:17)

What did Jesus teach about the Law of Moses? Did he say that he came to bring it to an end, or did he want his followers to obey it? Matthew 5:17-20 is a key passage that speaks to this question. In this passage, Jesus explains exactly what he came to do with the Law and Prophets. He said, "Do not think that I have come to abolish the Law or the Prophets; I have not come to abolish them but to fulfill them" (Matt. 5:17). In this chapter, we will explore what Jesus meant by the terms "abolish" and "fulfill."

### I Have Not Come to Abolish Them

Matthew 5:17-20 is part of Jesus's Sermon on the Mount (Matt. 5-7). Following the "Beatitudes" at the start of his sermon (Matt. 5:1-12), Jesus calls upon his followers to live as "salt" and "light" (Matt. 5:13-15) and exhibit "good works" so that the world will give glory to the Father (Matt. 5:16). The rest of the sermon elaborates on the nature of those good works, starting with Jesus's foundational statement about the Law in Matthew 5:17-20.[1] This passage offers crucial

---

[1] See Matthias Konradt: "The compositional placement of 5.17–20 as the opening of the body of the Sermon on the Mount and also as the first statement in the Gospel on the Torah and the Prophets already signals the great, indeed programmatic, significance that Matthew assigns to this verse" (*Christology, Torah, and Ethics in the Gospel of Matthew*, trans. Wayne Coppins [Waco, TX: Baylor University Press, 2022], 76).

insight into Jesus's perspective on the Law[2] and serves as Jesus's "thesis statement" regarding how his followers should relate to the Law.[3] As we will see in Chapters 3-4, Jesus expects his followers to obey and teach the Law better than the scribes and Pharisees (Matt. 5:19-20). His followers will exceed the Pharisees in righteousness by adhering to Jesus's proper interpretation of the Torah, which he articulates throughout the rest of the sermon (Matt. 5:21ff).

Jesus begins his statement on the Law by commanding his listeners to think correctly about his mission: "*Do not think* that I have come to abolish the Law or Prophets" (Matt. 5:17, emphasis added). Here, Jesus prohibits his listeners from even thinking that he came to abolish the Law or Prophets,[4] which implies that some of his listeners thought that he *did* come to abolish them.[5] This command against incorrect thinking is perhaps intended to address the scribes and Pharisees, who repeatedly accuse Jesus and his disciples of disregarding the Law (e.g., Matt. 12:1-14).[6] Jesus's statement in Matthew 5:17 directly

---

2   See Steven James Stiles: "there is essential agreement that Matthew 5:17 serves a programmatic function in the Gospel, that is, it provides a key to understanding the Matthean Jesus' attitude towards the Torah" (*Jesus' Fulfilment of the Torah and Prophets* [Tübingen: Mohr Siebeck, 2023], 2).

3   Craig Keener, *The Gospel of Matthew: A Socio-Rhetorical Commentary* (Grand Rapids, MI: Eerdmans, 2009), 175. See also George A. Kennedy, who says Matthew 5:17-20 serves "as the proposition of the sermon" (*New Testament Interpretation Through Rhetorical Criticism* [Chapel Hill, NC: University of North Carolina Press, 1984], 54).

4   See David Turner: "Jesus's disciples are forbidden to think that he has come to abolish the law" (*Matthew*, BECNT [Grand Rapids, MI: Baker Academic, 2008], 162).

5   See Donald A. Hagner: "'do not think that I came,' presupposes the existence of the opinion that is denied" (*Matthew*, WBC 33A [Dallas, TX: Word, 1993], 1:104).

6   Keener, 176; J. A. Overman, *Matthew's Gospel and Formative Judaism: The Social World of the Matthean Community* (Minneapolis, MN: Fortress Press, 1990), 88. See also Graham Stanton: "We know that Jewish opponents of Christianity frequently alleged that Jesus and his followers had abandoned the law, and we know that in several passages

refutes such accusations.[7] As Noel Rabinowitz explains, Jesus's prohibition against thinking that he came to abolish the Law is intended to confront "the charge that he has abandoned the Torah of Moses" and reassure his listeners that he "was not guilty of antinomianism."[8] Thus, believing that Jesus came to abolish the Law violates Jesus's command in Matthew 5:17—his listeners are *not even to think* that he came to do that.

What did Jesus mean by the "Law and Prophets"? This phrase refers to the Hebrew Scriptures or "Old Testament."[9] However, within the didactic context of Jesus's sermon, the terms "Law" and "Prophets" also have a legal connotation.[10] When Jesus says that he did not come

---

Matthew is responding to Jewish counter-propaganda. So is it not probable that the scribes and Pharisees who are in view in 5.20 at the end of this pericope are also in view at the beginning of 5.17? In this verse the evangelist opens his sustained exposition of his case concerning the Scriptures: 'Don't think, as the scribes and Pharisees allege, that I have come to destroy the law and the prophets...' For Matthew the law and the prophets continue to be authoritative for Christians" (*A Gospel for a New People: Studies in Matthew* [Edinburgh: T&T Clark, 1992], 49).

7   See Stiles, 82: "Matthew takes the accusation of καταλύω ['abolish'] very seriously and makes sure that it is refuted with the very first thing Jesus says about the Torah."

8   Noel Rabinowitz, "Yes, the Torah is Fulfilled, But What Does This Mean? An Exegetical Exposition," *Kesher: A Journal of Messianic Judaism* 11 (2000), 21.

9   See Craig Evans: "In this context, 'the law and the prophets' refers to the entirety of Jewish Scripture" (*Matthew*, NCBC [New York, NY: Cambridge University Press, 2012], 114). Evans cites the Wisdom of ben Sira, 2 Macc. 15:9, 4 Macc. 18:10, and b.*Ta'anit* 17b, 20a.

10  According to Hans Dieter Betz, these terms "are to be construed primarily as legal terms." So, even though the term "Law" (νόμος) refers to the Pentateuch (Genesis-Deuteronomy) as Scripture, Jesus uses it as "a legal term referring to the Mosaic Torah and its binding authority." Similarly, the term "Prophets" (προφήτης) refers "to the Old Testament prophetic books in their capacity as binding legal authority; they are in this sense also law" (*The Sermon on the Mount: A Commentary on the Sermon on the Mount, including the Sermon on the Plain (Matthew 5:3-7:27 and Luke 6:20-49)*, Hermeneia

to abolish the Law, he isn't talking about abolishing the Law's existence; he is talking about abolishing the Law's *legal authority*.[11] Jesus did not come to abolish the authority of the Law or the Prophets.

But what exactly did Jesus mean when he said that he did not come to *abolish*? To "abolish" (καταλύω) something means "to cause [it] to be no longer in force."[12] So, to abolish the Law and Prophets means to "do away with, annul or repeal" them.[13] In other words, Jesus forbids his listeners from thinking that he came to nullify or repeal God's commandments found in the Law and Prophets.

Several first-century Jewish texts give us additional insight into what it means to abolish the Law.[14] Like Matthew 5:17-20, these Jewish texts employ the term καταλύω ("abolish," Matt. 5:17) and the related term λύω ("relaxes," Matt. 5:19) in reference to the Law. For instance, 4 Maccabees 17:9 characterizes Antiochus as "the tyrant who wished to abolish [καταλῦσαι] the way of life of the Hebrews."[15] Moreover, in 4 Maccabees 5, there is an account of Antiochus attempting to compel the priest Eleazer to eat pork. Eleazer refuses, insisting that eating prohibited meats "is an abolishment [καταλῦσαι] of the ancestral law" (4 Macc. 5:33).[16] Josephus similarly writes that Antiochus "put pressure upon the Jews to abolish [καταλύσαντας]

---

[Minneapolis, MN: Fortress Press, 1995], 177-178).

11   Ibid., 178.

12   Walter Bauer, *A Greek-English Lexicon of the New Testament and Other Early Christian Literature*, rev. and ed. Frederick W. Danker, 4th ed. (Chicago: University of Chicago Press, 2021), 462.

13   Ibid. See also Keener, 177: to abolish the Law "was to cast of its yoke, treating God's law as void."

14   For a detailed examination of this literature, see Matthew Thiessen, "Abolishers of the Law in Early Judaism and Matthew 5, 17-20," *Biblica* 93, no. 4 (2012), 453-556.

15   Ibid., 547.

16   Ibid., 546.

their ancestral customs, leaving their infants uncircumcised and sacrificing swine upon the altar" (*Jewish Wars* 1.34).[17] These examples from Jewish literature show that to "abolish the Law" means to deny the Law's authority. Those who abolish the Law disregard the Law's commandments and encourage others to disregard them as well. The parallel in verse 19 confirms this meaning: "Therefore whoever relaxes [λύω] one of the least of these commandments and teaches others to do the same will be called least in the kingdom of heaven" (Matt. 5:19).

In sum, Jesus commands his listeners not to think that he came to invalidate the commandments in the Law and Prophets. He reassures them that, unlike Antiochus, this was not his purpose. Believing that Jesus came to nullify the commandments of the Torah breaks Jesus's commandment in Matthew 5:17 against thinking that he came to abolish the Law.

## Does Paul Teach that Jesus Abolished the Law?

Despite what Matthew 5:17 seems to say, some interpreters contend that this verse cannot mean that Jesus would never abolish the Law because Jesus eventually *did* abolish the Law. In Ephesians 2:15, Paul explicitly states that Jesus "abolish[ed] the law of commandments expressed in ordinances."[18] According to R. L. Solberg, the expression

---

17  Ibid., 547.

18  See, e.g., John MacArthur, *Ephesians*, The MacArthur New Testament Commentary (Chicago, IL: Moody Press, 1986), 77. MacArthur reconciles these two passages by arguing that Matthew 5:17 refers only to "God's moral law" and that Ephesians 2:15 refers to the "ceremonial law," but this suggestion seems contrived. Averbeck remarks that "the categories of moral, civil, and ceremonial law never appear in the Bible" and "are artificial and misleading." He further states, "As for myself, I am convinced that the threefold division is neither legitimate nor helpful, from a biblical point of view,

"law of commandments expressed in ordinances" in Ephesians 2:15 is "an unambiguous reference to the Mosaic Law."[19] Solberg further states, "And what does the text say Jesus did to that law? He abolished it."[20] So, in light of Ephesians 2:15, it is argued that we cannot interpret Matthew 5:17 as saying that Jesus will *never* abolish the Law of Moses. Jesus did not abolish the Torah during his earthly ministry; however, after his death, he *did* abolish it.[21]

This objection has significant problems. First, the very next verse in Matthew states that the whole Law will endure "until heaven and earth pass away" and "until all is accomplished" (Matt. 5:18). As I will demonstrate in Chapter 2, these two clauses refer to the same event: the end of the present age. Hence, no part of the Law could pass away prior to that future time.

The second problem with this objection is that it causes Paul to contradict not only Jesus but also himself. In Romans 3:31, Paul uses the same Greek word for "abolish" (καταργέω) that he uses in Ephesians 2:15. There, he declares that our faith does not abolish the Law

---

for resolving the issue of the application of the Old Testament law to the church and the believer." (*The Old Testament Law for the Life of the Church: Reading the Torah in Light of Christ* [Downers Grove, IL: IVP Academic, 2022], 13, 21-22). In their book on hermeneutics, J. Scott Duvall and J. Daniel Hays similarly remark that the approach of dividing the Law into these categories "is too ambiguous and too inconsistent to be a valid approach to interpreting Scripture. We simply do not see a clear distinction in Scripture between these different categories of law" (*Grasping God's Word: A Hands-On Approach to Reading, Interpreting, and Applying the Bible*, 3rd ed. [Grand Rapids, MI: Zondervan, 2012], 358).

19  R. L. Solberg, *Torahism: Are Christians Required to Keep the Law of Moses?* 2nd ed. (Franklin, TN: Williamson College Press, 2022), 86.
20  Ibid.
21  Like καταλύω, the term καταργέω in Ephesians 2:15 similarly means to "make ineffective, nullify" (Bauer, 465).

but rather establishes it. If Paul thought Jesus abolished the Law when he died on the cross, why does he say that the Law is not abolished in Romans 3:31?

As we continue reading through the Epistle to the Ephesians, a third problem with this objection becomes evident: Paul presupposes the validity of the Law. In Ephesians 6:1-3, Paul instructs children to obey their parents, and then directly quotes the Fifth Commandment to underpin this ethical instruction (cf. Exod. 20:12). It makes no sense for Paul to cite the Torah as authoritative if he considered it abolished.

Given the problems with the antinomian interpretation of Ephesians 2:15, how should we understand Paul's statement about Jesus "abolishing the law of commandments expressed in ordinances"? A closer examination of the specific words used in the verse resolves the issue. Contrary to Solberg, when Paul says "law" in this verse, he is not referring to the Law of Moses. This is evident because he does not just say "law"; instead, he says "law" with several qualifying terms: "of commandments" (τῶν ἐντολῶν) and "expressed in ordinances" (ἐν δόγμασιν). According to Lionel Windsor, these qualifying terms "perform a defining function: they specify what would otherwise be ambiguous."[22] That is, these terms define "law" in Ephesians 2:15 more specifically as a particular (mis)understanding and (mis)use of the Law.[23] In light of these qualifications in the text, it makes more sense to interpret the phrase "the law of commandments expressed in ordinances" in Ephesians 2:15 as referring to extrabiblical rulings and

---

22 Lionel J. Windsor, *Reading Ephesians and Colossians after Supersessionism: Christ's Mission Through Israel to the Nations* (Eugene, OR: Cascade Books, 2017), 136-137.

23 See Ibid., 137: "In other words, the qualifications indicate that what has been abolished is not necessarily the law in every sense, but rather the law as understood and used in a certain way: 'the law of the commandments in decrees.'"

teachings derived from a misunderstanding and misapplication of the Law of Moses.[24] Such man-made rules often created division between Jews and Gentiles (Eph. 2:14). For example, some Jewish leaders prohibited Jews and Gentiles eating together. The Torah never commands that Jews and Gentiles must eat separately, but Jewish texts like the book of Jubilees did (Jubilees 22:16). Some of the Jewish groups that disputed with the apostles held to this unbiblical and divisive "law" (Acts 11:3; Gal. 2:11-14). The whole context of Ephesians 2 is about having Jews and Gentiles worship together in harmony, and so the extrabiblical and divisive laws that hinder that harmony are what Paul is saying Christ abolished.[25] Thus, when interpreted correctly, Ephesians 2:15 does not contradict Jesus's statement in Matthew 5:17.

---

24  The word "commandments" (ἐντολή) refers to man-made commandments in John 11:57 and Acts 17:15. Moreover, the word "ordinances" (δόγμα) always refers to man-made traditions or ordinances (e.g., Luke 2:1; Acts 16:4; 17:7; LXX Esther 4:8; 9:1; Daniel 6:12). See Windsor, 136-140. See also Gregory Scott McKenzie, "Pronomian Paradigm: A Pro-Torah, Christocentric Method of Theology and Apologetics" (Ph.D. diss., Liberty University, 2024), 123-125, https://digitalcommons.liberty.edu/doctoral/5623/.

25  See Windsor, 139: "[W]hat has been abolished is the law understood primarily as a set of 'commandments' as expressed and promulgated by certain authoritative 'decrees' concerning the observance of these commandments. The law understood in this way had indeed produced hostility between Jews and gentiles—as illustrated by the officially sanctioned inscription at the dividing-wall in the temple. This is what Paul is claiming to have been abolished by Christ. Paul is not denigrating the law itself, nor is he ruling out any possible attempt to apply the law to the lives of believers." See also Klyne R. Snodgrass: "Paul does not abolish the law as the Word of God or as a moral guide (cf. his quoting one of the ten commandments in 6:2). What is abolished is the law as a set of regulations that excludes Gentiles" (*Ephesians*, NIVAC [Grand Rapids, MI: Zondervan, 1996], 133).

## I Have Come to Fulfill Them

Instead of disregarding or nullifying the Law and Prophets, Jesus said he came to fulfill them: "I have not come to abolish them but to fulfill them" (Matt. 5:17). What does it mean "to fulfill" the Law and Prophets? Depending upon the context, the verb "to fulfill" (πληρόω) can mean to carry out, to show forth true meaning, or to complete.[26] So, which of these definitions best fits the context? Did Jesus come to carry out the Law and Prophets, to show the true meaning of the Law and Prophets, or to complete the Law and Prophets?

In this context, the statement that Jesus came to fulfill the Law and Prophets is situated between his exhortations to perform good works (Matt. 5:16)[27] and to do and teach the commandments (Matt. 5:19). Moreover, the overall focus of Matthew 5–7 is "on the teaching of Jesus and is intended to be didactic in function."[28] It would seem, then, that the sense of "fully doing" or "revealing true meaning" fits this context better than the idea of "completing." Consequently, in Matthew 5:17, fulfilling the Law and Prophets should be understood as fully doing and teaching them, corresponding to Matthew 5:19 ("whoever does them and teaches them"). Indeed, just as "relaxes" in verse 19 parallels "abolish" in verse 17, "does and teaches" in verse 19 parallels "fulfill" in verse 17. In other words, Jesus fulfills the Law and Prophets by teaching and demonstrating the proper way to observe them as God intended.[29] Steven Stiles puts it well: "πληρόω ['to

---

26   Bauer, 736. See also Turner, 157.
27   See Turner, 162: "To Matthew's Christian Jewish audience, 'good works' (5:16) would imply righteous works (מִצְווֹת, *miswôt*) enjoined by the law and the prophets."
28   J. Daryl Charles, "Garnishing with the 'Greater Righteousness': The Disciple's Relationship to the Law (Matthew 5:17-20)," *Bulletin for Biblical Research* 12, no. 1 (2002), 9.
29   See Hagner, 106: "Since in 5:21-48 Jesus defines righteousness by expounding the true meaning of the law as opposed to wrong or shallow understandings, it is best to

fulfill'] carries the idea of fulfilling or doing a requirement or religious obligation to its fullest. In the case of Matthew 5:17, it has to do with being completely obedient to the Torah and teaching it properly."[30]

However, some interpreters disagree with this understanding of "to fulfill" and argue that, in Matthew 5:17, the verb instead carries the meaning of "bring to completion." According to this interpretation, Jesus came to "fulfill" the Law and Prophets by satisfying their prophetic predictions.[31] As we saw in the introduction, proponents of this understanding include R. L. Solberg and Andy Stanley. Solberg contends that when Jesus said he came to fulfill the Law and Prophets, he was referring to fulfilling the Messianic types and prophecies within them, particularly those predicting his death on the cross: "Jesus indeed came 'not to abolish but fulfill' what the Law required. And what did the Law require? A perfect sacrifice for sin."[32] And since the Messiah's death on the cross "fulfilled what the Torah was pointing toward," this means that "Christians today are not bound by the legal

---

understand πληρῶσαι here as 'fulfill' in the sense of 'bring to its intended meaning'—that is, to present a definitive interpretation of the law." See also David C. Sim: "Jesus the Messiah provides the authoritative and definitive exegesis of the law; he fulfills the law by bringing out its original intention and meaning" (*The Gospel of Matthew and Christian Judaism: The History and Social Setting of the Matthean Community* [Edinburgh: T&T Clark Ltd, 1998], 124).

30  Stiles, 80. See also Charles, 3: "Most interpreters of Matthew acknowledge that Jesus is not a new law-giver but *the* legitimate interpreter of the divine will as contained in the Torah and reiterated by the prophets."

31  Many note that Matthew often uses πληρόω to speak of the Messiah "fulfilling" biblical prophecy (e.g., Matt. 2:17, 23; 4:14; 13:14; 26:56; 27:9). See Solberg, 130: "what does it mean for Jesus to fulfill the Hebrew Scriptures? It means satisfying everything that spoke of Him or pointed to Him, including the messianic prophecies. The theme of fulfillment is all over the New Testament."

32  Solberg, 157.

requirements of the Law of Moses."³³ Similarly, Andy Stanley remarks, "Jesus did not abolish the law when he fulfilled it. But in fulfilling it, he made it...obsolete."³⁴ In addition to Solberg and Stanley, Matthew Vines goes to the extent of arguing that continuing to obey the Torah after Jesus "fulfilled" it diminishes Jesus's work on the cross: "Once Christ fulfilled the law, his followers would have trivialized his sacrifice by living as though they were still subject to the law's constraints."³⁵ Hence, according to these interpreters, fulfilling the Law results in the Law coming to an end.

But did Jesus really make the Law of Moses obsolete by fulfilling it? Even if we grant the assumption that "to fulfill" in Matthew 5:17 means to fulfill the prophetic symbols and predictions found in the Law and Prophets, there are several problems with the idea that this somehow results in the Law coming to an end. The biggest problem with this idea is that it sounds exactly like what Jesus said he did not come to do. There is no difference between abolishing something and making it obsolete; the result is the same. And since Jesus contrasts "fulfill" (πληρόω) with "abolish" (καταλύω), these words cannot mean the same thing.³⁶

---

33  Ibid.
34  Andy Stanley, *Irresistible: Reclaiming the New that Jesus Unleashed for the World* (Grand Rapids, MI: Zondervan, 2018), 110.
35  Matthew Vines, *God and the Gay Christian: The Biblical Case in Support of Same-Sex Relationships* (Convergent Books, 2014), 199. See also Solberg, 51, who similarly argues that the notion that Christians should keep the Law "undermines the accomplishments of Jesus through His life, death, and resurrection."
36  See Charles, 8: "While much exegetical ink has been spilled in attempts to render precisely the verbs *plerosai* ('fulfill') and *katalysai* ('abrogate,' 'loose' or 'annul'), understanding the context in which they appear as well as their proper relationship to each other—one of *contrast*—is critical to their proper sense in Matt 5:17. The nature of the actions is antithesis and mutual exclusion." See also Benjamin John Stepan Szumskyj: "if one's

## What it Means to Fulfill the Law (Matthew 5:17)

Additionally, if we apply this logic consistently, we could reasonably conclude that many other practices that most Christians believe we should observe have become obsolete. For instance, Jesus's death and resurrection "fulfilled" the symbolism of Baptism (Rom. 6:3-4), but nobody believes that Baptism is now obsolete and that we shouldn't baptize new believers. During the Last Supper, Jesus said that the bread and wine pointed toward his work of redemption (Luke 22:19-20). Jesus then "fulfilled" what they pointed toward, but nobody concludes from this that Christians shouldn't partake in the bread and wine.[37] Hence, why should we think that Jesus "fulfilling" the Law and Prophets through his work on the cross renders them irrelevant for Christian practice?

Finally, as I will discuss in further detail in Chapters 2 and 3, the immediate context further complicates this interpretation. Jesus continues his statement on the Law and Prophets by announcing that nothing will pass from the Law until heaven and earth pass away (Matt. 5:18) and warns against disregarding the commandments of the Law (Matt. 5:19). It makes little sense to insist upon keeping the

---

definition of 'fulfill' results in abolishment, then Jesus' statement is an oxymoron" ("The Role of the Law in the Sanctification of the Believer Today: A Brief Introduction to Pronomianism" (Ph.D. diss., Liberty University, 2024), 269, https://digitalcommons.liberty.edu/doctoral/5479/).

37  Although the communion meal was practiced by Christians very early on, since the original context of Jesus's instructions to "do this in remembrance of me" is the Passover meal, I do not think Jesus was instituting a new ritual. I think he was telling his disciples to observe Passover in remembrance of him. Nevertheless, the argument still applies whether one partakes in the bread and wine during a communion ceremony or only once a year during Passover. For a paper that argues that Jesus and Paul were instructing the early Christians to observe the annual Passover rather than a distinct communion ritual, see Tim Hegg, "An Investigation of 'The Lord's Table,'" in *Celebrate the Feast: Collected Articles on the Spring Festivals* (Tacoma, WA: TorahResource, 2019), 93-112.

Torah and warn about the consequences of breaking the Torah if the Torah itself is about to become irrelevant.

In contrast to Solberg and Stanley, it is best to understand "I came to fulfill the Law and Prophets" as "I came to bring out the *full meaning* of the Law and Prophets." Jesus fulfills the Law and Prophets by teaching and demonstrating how to obey them properly. Not only does this meaning of "fulfill" fit the context much better than the idea of fulfilling prophecy, but it also provides an actual contrast with the word "abolish." It seems strange for Jesus to contrast the notion of nullifying the Torah's commandments with the idea of fulfilling prophecy. But it makes perfect sense for Jesus to contrast the notion of nullifying the Torah's commandments with the idea of *affirming* them.

## Conclusion

In Matthew 5:17, Jesus announces that he did not come to abolish the Law or Prophets. In fact, he explicitly commands us *not even to think* that he came to do that. Instead, he says that he came to *fulfill* them. Considering the context, the verb "to fulfill" (πληρόω) in this verse does not mean to bring to completion in the sense of fulfilling prophecy, nor does this term imply that Jesus made the Law obsolete. Rather, Jesus coming "to fulfill" the Law and Prophets means that he came to confirm the authority of the Law and the Prophets through his teachings and actions. He came to reveal the true meaning of the Law and Prophets by teaching and demonstrating how to obey them properly.

CHAPTER 2

# UNTIL HEAVEN AND EARTH PASS AWAY
## (MATTHEW 5:18)

After announcing that he did not come to abolish the Law and Prophets but to fulfill them, Jesus goes on to declare that the whole Torah will remain relevant as long as heaven and earth exist. In other words, it will not be going away any time soon. In this chapter, we will delve into the significance of Jesus's statement that nothing will pass from the Law "until heaven and earth pass away" and "until all is accomplished."

## The Smallest Details of the Law Remain

In Matthew 5:18, Jesus says, "For truly, I say to you, until heaven and earth pass away, not an iota, not a dot, will pass from the Law until all is accomplished" (Matt. 5:18). According to this verse, the smallest details of the Torah[1] are essential, and not a single letter will pass away until a future time—that is, "until heaven and earth pass away" and "until all is accomplished." According to David Turner, these two temporal clauses are "essentially synonymous references to the end of the present world and the beginning of the eschaton. Until that time

---

[1] See Noel Rabinowitz: "The iota (ι) is the smallest letter of the Greek alphabet and here represents its Hebrew equivalent, the letter yodh (י). Κεραια literally means 'horn' or 'hook' and refers to the small writing stroke used to distinguish between similar letters... This expression is a metaphor and refers to the smallest detail or part of the Torah" ("Yes, the Torah is Fulfilled, But What Does This Mean? An Exegetical Exposition," *Kesher: A Journal of Messianic Judaism* 11 [2000], 30).

the law is valid."[2] Scripture elsewhere describes the end of the present world as heaven and earth passing away and as God establishing a new heaven and earth. Peter wrote that "the heavens and earth that now exist are stored up for fire, being kept until the day of judgment and destruction of the ungodly" and that "we are waiting for new heavens and a new earth in which righteousness dwells" (2 Pet. 3:7, 13). He further states that "the day of the Lord will come like a thief, and then the heavens will pass away" (2 Pet. 3:10). Similarly, in his vision of the future New Jerusalem, John states that the present heaven and earth will pass away and be replaced by a new heaven and a new earth (Rev. 21:1; cf. Isa. 65:17; 66:22). In a passage reminiscent of Matthew 5:18, the first-century Jewish teacher Philo similarly taught that the whole Torah would remain "as long as the sun and the moon, and the whole heaven and the whole world shall endure" (Philo, *Life of Moses* 2:14). Jesus's original listeners would have grasped his point clearly: the entire Law remains binding until God establishes a new heaven and earth after the present fallen world has completely passed away. As Turner writes, "It would be hard to make a stronger statement of the ongoing authority of the Torah than that made in 5:18."[3]

In contrast to this view, some interpret the second temporal clause in Matthew 5:18 ("until all is accomplished") as referring to the Messiah's death and resurrection. According to this interpretation, Jesus states that the Law of Moses will remain in effect only until he com-

---

2   David Turner, *Matthew*, BECNT (Grand Rapids, MI: Baker Academic, 2008), 163. See also Donald A. Hagner, *Matthew*, WBC 33A (Dallas, TX: Word, 1993), 1:107-108; Matthias Konradt: "the two ἕως phrases in Matt 5.18b, d are materially identical. No iota or stroke will pass away as long as this world exists" (*Christology, Torah, and Ethics in the Gospel of Matthew*, trans. Wayne Coppins [Waco, TX: Baylor University Press, 2022], 78).

3   Turner, 163.

pletes his work on the cross, after which it should be discarded. As Andy Stanley remarks, "According to Jesus, nothing in the law would 'disappear' until everything was 'accomplished.' Once it was accomplished, however, the law would begin to disappear. Which is exactly what happened."[4] Solberg echoes Stanley, arguing that all was already accomplished at the cross: "Jesus taught that not an 'iota or a dot' shall pass from the Law until all is accomplished. And then He taught that all had been accomplished. The Mosaic Law was always intended to be temporary; its divine expiration date was the arrival of Jesus."[5]

However, is this a plausible interpretation of Matthew 5:18? Was Jesus really implying that the Torah would remain in effect only until he finished his work on the cross? According to Craig Keener, the interpretation proposed by Stanley and Solberg "violates the whole thrust of the passage."[6] J. Andrew Overman similarly remarks, "Such hermeneutical gymnastics seem excessive, if not tortured."[7] The most obvious problem with interpreting the second clause as a reference to the moment Christ accomplished his work on the cross is that it "plainly contradicts the meaning of the first clause, which refers to the ongoing validity of the law until the end of the age."[8] A second problem with this interpretation of Matthew 5:18 is that it contradicts Matthew 5:17. As David Sim explains, "If the Matthean Jesus claims in 5:18 that

---

4  Andy Stanley, *Irresistible: Reclaiming the New that Jesus Unleashed for the World* (Grand Rapids, MI: Zondervan, 2018), 111.

5  R. L. Solberg, *Torahism: Are Christians Required to Keep the Law of Moses?* 2nd ed. (Franklin, TN: Williamson College Press, 2022), 157.

6  Craig Keener, *The Gospel of Matthew: A Socio-Rhetorical Commentary* (Grand Rapids, MI: Eerdmans, 2009), 178.

7  J. Andrew Overman, *Church and Community in Crisis: The Gospel According to Matthew* (Valley Forge, PA: Trinity Press International, 1996), 77.

8  Hagner, 107.

the law does become invalid with his death or resurrection, then he obviously did come to abolish the law, and this is a patent contradiction of what he says in the preceding verse."[9] Finally, a third problem is that this interpretation is inconsistent with Matthew 5:19. It seems strange that Jesus would warn his followers against disregarding the commandments and strongly emphasize the importance of obeying and teaching them if the Law was soon to become obsolete.

Considering the significant problems with interpreting the second clause ("until all is accomplished") as being a reference to the Messiah's death and resurrection, it is more appropriate to view it as synonymous with the first clause ("until heaven and earth pass away"). Thus, when Jesus states that nothing will pass from the Law until all is accomplished, he means that nothing will pass from the Law "until the consummation of the kingdom, when heaven and earth pass away."[10] This implies that the Torah in its entirety—even the "least" commandment (Matt. 5:19; 23:23)—remains in force.

## But Have Things Already Passed From the Law?

Despite this straightforward reading of Mathew 5:18, Solberg insists that Jesus could not have meant what he said in this verse. He writes, "Jesus could not have meant there would be no change in the Law until heaven and earth pass away."[11] Solberg rejects the notion that the Torah will endure until heaven and earth pass away because, as he puts it, *"some things have already passed from the law."*[12] Then, Solberg goes on to mention a few examples of commandments that

---

9    David C. Sim, *The Gospel of Matthew and Christian Judaism: The History and Social Setting of the Matthean Community* (Edinburgh: T&T Clark Ltd, 1998), 125.
10   Keener, 178.
11   Solberg, 143.
12   Ibid., 131. Emphasis in original.

he believes have already passed from the Law based on how he interprets certain passages in Hebrews and Paul's epistles.[13] In other words, Solberg approaches Matthew 5:18 with a predetermined conclusion about what the text is allowed to say. Since Jesus "could not have meant" that the Torah will remain binding until heaven and earth pass away, Solberg resorts to *changing* Jesus's words to make the verse say something different. He writes, "Jesus meant something like: *the following statement shall remain true until heaven and earth pass away: nothing will pass from the law until all is accomplished.*"[14]

It is my contention that drawing a conclusion about Matthew 5:18 from unrelated passages and then modifying the text of Matthew 5:18 to fit your presuppositions is not a sound interpretive approach.[15] Shouldn't we seek to understand Matthew 5:18 for what it says within its own context?[16] Nevertheless, there is indeed more to the Bible than

---

13  Ibid., 131-143.

14  Ibid., 143. Solberg offers another interpretation of Jesus's statement in Matthew 5:18 as an additional option, again changing the words of the verse to state, "Sooner Heaven and Earth would pass away than I will fail to fulfill what the Scriptures foretold" (142). Both of Solberg's interpretive suggestions rely upon adding and rearranging words in the verse, which strikes me as problematic. If Jesus meant what Solberg suggests he means, why would he express this meaning in such a confusing way?

15  In his book on Biblical interpretation, Walter C. Kaiser warns against using the whole canon of Scripture to usurp "the place of the author in the exegetical procedure." The rest of Scripture can be consulted for fuller context only *after* "we have finished our exegetical work of establishing what, indeed, the author of the paragraph or text under consideration was trying to say." Kaiser insists that "canonical context must appear only as part of our summation and not as part of our exegesis" (*Toward an Exegetical Theology: Biblical Exegesis for Preaching and Teaching* [Grand Rapids, MI: Baker Book House, 1981], 82-83).

16  See J. Scott Duvall and J. Daniel Hays: "We study literary context because the interpretation that best fits the context is the most valid interpretation. When we disregard literary context, we run the risk of forcing the Bible to say what we want it to say" (*Grasping*

## Until Heaven and Earth Pass Away (Matthew 5:18)

Matthew 5:18, and we must take all Scripture into consideration as we build our theology. When it comes to harmonizing seemingly conflicting passages, however, I would propose that a better approach is to prioritize clearer passages over ambiguous passages. In this case, Matthew 5:18 is an example of a clear passage. As Overman writes, "Although this passage is the subject of lively controversy, it is unambiguous and does indeed command obedience to the whole Torah."[17] In contrast, the passages that Solberg uses to support his conclusion are more complex and prone to misinterpretation (e.g., 2 Pet. 3:15-17).[18] Hence, if we aim to reconcile these passages, the clear text of Matthew 5:18 should serve as our reference point while examining the more ambiguous texts in Hebrews and Paul's epistles, rather than using the ambiguous texts to interpret Matthew 5:18.

In this book's appendix, I will offer an alternative interpretation of the passages that Solberg uses to argue that certain commandments have passed from the Torah. I will demonstrate that the antinomian reading of these passages is erroneous and that a *pronomian* reading is more consistent not only with a straightforward interpretation of Matthew 5:18 but also with the context of each of these passages on their own. However, for our current purposes, I will simply state that the antinomian readings of unrelated passages should not be used to distort the clear meaning of Matthew 5:18.

---

*God's Word: A Hands-On Approach to Reading, Interpreting, and Applying the Bible*, 3rd ed. [Grand Rapids, MI: Zondervan, 2012] 161).

17 Overman, 78.

18 See Matthew Thiessen: "2 Peter states (perspicuously, I might add) that it is Paul's letters themselves that are, at least in places, obscure and therefore challenging to interpret. And it is their very obscurity that makes them susceptible to misuse and to being twisted" (*A Jewish Paul: The Messiah's Herald to the Gentiles* [Grand Rapids, MI: Baker Academic, 2023], 1-2).

## Conclusion

In Matthew 5:18, Jesus states that nothing will pass from the Law until heaven and earth pass away and all is accomplished, which means that nothing will pass from the Law until the end of the present world. While some have argued that "until all is accomplished" refers to the Messiah's death and resurrection, the text precludes this option because (1) it would cause the second part of verse 18 to contradict the first part, (2) it would cause verse 18 to contradict verse 17, and (3) such an interpretation is inconsistent with verse 19. Hence, the second clause in verse 18 ("until all is accomplished") should be viewed as synonymous with the first clause ("until heaven and earth pass away"). According to Jesus, as long as heaven and earth exist, the whole Torah will remain binding.

CHAPTER 3

# DO AND TEACH THE COMMANDMENTS
## (MATTHEW 5:19)

In the previous verse, Jesus said that the whole Law of Moses will remain in effect for as long as heaven and earth exist. Now, in Matthew 5:19, he insists that his followers should therefore be keeping it. As Dale Allison writes, "Matthew 5:19 elaborates on 5:18 in a way reminiscent of how the latter elaborates on 5:17: if all of the law remains in force, then all of the law must be obeyed."[1] In this chapter, we will unpack Jesus's warning against disregarding the Torah's commandments and his call to be great in the kingdom by doing and teaching the Torah's commandments.

## Whoever Relaxes vs. Whoever Does and Teaches

In Matthew 5:19, Jesus warns against "relaxing" the commandments. He urges his followers to be great in the kingdom of heaven by doing and teaching the commandments:

> Therefore whoever relaxes one of the least of these commandments and teaches others to do the same will be called least in the kingdom of heaven, but whoever does them and teaches them will be called great in the kingdom of heaven.
> —Matthew 5:19

---

[1] Dale C. Allison, *The Sermon on the Mount: Inspiring the Moral Imagination* (New York, NY: Crossroad, 1999), 60.

## Do and Teach the Commandments (Matthew 5:19)

What did Jesus mean when he warned against relaxing the commandments? The Greek word for "relaxes" (λύω) in this verse is related to the word "abolish" (καταλύω) in Matthew 5:17, and it similarly carries the sense of "repeal, annul, abolish."[2] Essentially, Jesus says that since *he* did not come to nullify or disregard the Law of Moses (Matt. 5:17), neither should his followers (Matt. 5:19). In fact, Jesus goes on to say that one's status in the kingdom—whether one will be "great" or "least"—is determined by whether one obeys and teaches the least of the commandments.

What does it mean to be "great" or "least" in the kingdom? This notion of greater and lesser status within the kingdom is discussed elsewhere in Matthew's Gospel (Matt: 5:12; 10:41-42; 11:11; 18:1-4; 20:16, 26), and it does not imply that the one who disregards the least of the commandments will be excluded from the kingdom entirely. Rather, Jesus is talking about heavenly rewards (or lack thereof).[3] As Noel Rabinowitz writes, "To be least in the Kingdom therefore means to receive little or no reward in the Kingdom. These are individuals who have remained faithful to the Torah—but just barely."[4] In contrast, the one who does and teaches the commandments will be "great"—he will receive more heavenly rewards. Thus, in the strongest terms, Matthew 5:19 emphasizes that followers of Jesus must not dismiss any aspect of

---

2 Walter Bauer, *A Greek-English Lexicon of the New Testament and Other Early Christian Literature*, rev. and ed. Frederick W. Danker, 4th ed. (Chicago: University of Chicago Press, 2021), 538.

3 See Matthias Konradt: "access to the kingdom of God is not blocked for the person who neglects small commandments or even declares them to be obsolete in their teaching, but the person will receive less honor there" (*Christology, Torah, and Ethics in the Gospel of Matthew*, trans. Wayne Coppins [Waco, TX: Baylor University Press, 2022], 79).

4 Noel Rabinowitz, "Yes, the Torah is Fulfilled, But What Does This Mean? An Exegetical Exposition," *Kesher: A Journal of Messianic Judaism* 11 (2000), 36.

the Law as insignificant; the whole Law remains valid and authoritative. As Craig Keener writes, "Jesus' point in 5:19 is the same as that of other Bible teachers in his day: one cannot pick and choose among the commandments but must obey them all."[5]

## Which Commandments?

When Jesus mentions the "commandments" in Matthew 5:19, is he referring to the Torah's commandments? Some interpreters argue that the "commandments" to be obeyed and taught in Matthew 5:19 refer not to those found in the Law of Moses but instead refer to "Christ's own instructions."[6] In other words, Jesus is not urging his followers to obey and teach the Torah; he is urging them to obey and teach his own distinct commandments that he issues throughout his sermon. These interpreters often cite the so-called "antitheses" in Matthew 5:21-48 ("you have heard it said…but I tell you") in support of this notion, imagining that Jesus sets up his own teachings in opposition to the Law of Moses. As Robert Banks argues, "The antitheses themselves are primarily directed at the Mosaic Law."[7]

---

5   Craig Keener, *The Gospel of Matthew: A Socio-Rhetorical Commentary* (Grand Rapids, MI: Eerdmans, 2009), 179. See also J. Daryl Charles: "All commandments have the same goal: loving God and loving others. All are binding, even when they have different 'weights' (see 23:23-24). Through teaching and practicing the law, it is 'affirmed,' 'confirmed,' and 'upheld.' The continuing validity of the law as an ethical guide is hereby emphasized" ("Garnishing with the 'Greater Righteousness': The Disciple's Relationship to the Law [Matthew 5:17-20]," *Bulletin for Biblical Research* 12, no. 1 [2002], 19).
6   Robert Banks, "Matthew's Understanding of the Law: Authenticity and Interpretation in Matthew 5:17-20," *JBL* 93 (1974), 240. See also Eduard Schweizer: "Probably the saying…refers to the commandments taught by Jesus, which follow" (*The Good News according to Matthew* [London: SPCK, 1976], 108-109).
7   Banks, 242.

However, does the context support the idea that Jesus is introducing new commandments that are separate from and contrary to those found in the Torah? Not at all. First, as Rabinowitz points out, the term "Law" (νόμος) in the previous verse is the antecedent of the word "these" (τούτων) in verse 19.[8] So, when Jesus refers to "these commandments," he is talking about the commandments contained in the Law of Moses that he just mentioned one verse earlier. Moreover, in Matthew's Gospel, the word "commandment" (ἐντολή) consistently pertains to the Law of Moses (e.g., Matt. 15:3; 19:17). Hence, interpreters should assume that it means the same thing in Matthew 5:19.[9] Finally, as Steven Stiles argues, the "least" of the commandments refers back to the "iotas and dots" in verse 18, and the term "relaxes" refers back to "abolish" in verse 17.[10] So, the Law from verses 17 and 18 is the same as the commandments from verse 19. Therefore, in light of the context, the phrase "these commandments" in Matthew 5:19 is best understood as a reference to the commandments found in the Law of Moses.[11]

---

8   Rabinowitz, 34.
9   Ibid. See also Steven James Stiles: "Elsewhere in Matthew's Gospel the noun ἐντολή always refers to commandments of the Torah (Matt 15:3; 19:17; 22:36, 40)" (*Jesus' Fulfilment of the Torah and Prophets* [Tübingen: Mohr Siebeck, 2023], 120).
10  See Stiles, 120: "'least' (ἐλαχίστων) harkens back to the minutiae mentioned in 5:18 (ἰῶτα ἓν ἢ μία κεραία) and 'loose' (λύω) recalls abolish (καταλύω) in 5:17."
11  See also Donald A. Hagner: "in keeping with the emphasis of the preceding verses, it is more naturally taken as a reference to the Mosaic law, and the equivalent of the 'jot and tittle' of v 18 (the majority of commentators)" (*Matthew*, WBC 33A [Dallas, TX: Word, 1993], 1:108). Surprisingly, even R. L. Solberg admits that this interpretation is most likely: "Some Christians suggest the phrase 'these commandments' refers to the commands Jesus is about to give his audience beginning in Matthew 5:21. But I don't believe that is the best interpretation. First, because in Matthew, the Greek word οὗτος (*houtos*, meaning 'this' or 'these') never points forward. But more importantly, verse 19 begins with the word 'therefore.' It is a conclusion based on the previous two verses. Jesus

## Understanding "the Antitheses"

Do Jesus's antithetical sayings in Matthew 5:21-48 contradict the Torah? If so, wouldn't this suggest that he is introducing his own "commandments" to replace the Law of Moses? While a few interpreters have made this argument, Jesus's statement in Matthew 5:17 makes such an interpretation impossible.[12] As we learned in Chapter 1, Jesus explicitly prohibits his listeners from thinking that his teachings abolish the Law. He said that he did *not* come to nullify the Law or Prophets. If we interpret Matthew 5:21-48 to mean that Jesus is pitting his own teachings against the teachings of the Torah, then we are violating his direct order in verse 17, when he said that we shouldn't think that he came to abolish the Law and the Prophets.

If Jesus is not contrasting his teachings with the Law of Moses in Matthew 5:21-48, what exactly is he contrasting them with? According to Stiles, Jesus's antithetical sayings are "directed at the interpretation of the scribes and Pharisees."[13] That is, Jesus is not opposing the Torah itself; rather, he is opposing the scribes' and Pharisees' inferior teachings on the Torah. As Stiles explains, "when the Matthean Jesus refers to what the crowds have 'heard' (ἠκούσατε), he is quoting the Torah as it is insufficiently interpreted by the scribes and Pharisees. This 'distorted' interpretation of the Torah produces a righteousness that is insufficient

---

is saying, 'Because nothing shall pass from the Law until all is accomplished...whoever relaxes one of the least of these commandments...' etc. So 'these commands' most likely refers to the Torah commands, none of which shall pass until all is accomplished" (*Torahism: Are Christians Required to Keep the Law of Moses?* 2nd ed. [Franklin, TN: Williamson College Press, 2022], 147).

12  See Craig Evans: "Jesus can hardly claim to fulfill the Law (Matt 5:17) if he then contradicts it" (*Matthew*, NCBC [New York, NY: Cambridge University Press, 2012], 120-121.

13  Stiles, 113.

for entering the kingdom of Heaven (Matt 5:20)."[14] Jesus condemns the inadequate righteousness of the Pharisees in verse 20, right before he starts into his teachings in verses 21-48. He then follows those teachings with another condemnation of the Pharisees' "righteousness" in Matthew 6:1-18. As Stiles remarks, "the antitheses are sandwiched between polemics against the scribes and Pharisees."[15] It is clear that Jesus is contrasting his teachings with the Pharisees' teachings, not with the Law and the Prophets.

As Jesus demonstrates in his antithetical sayings, the scribes and Pharisees are the ones who abolish the Torah (cf. Matt. 5:17). Through their hypocrisy and disregard for the commandments, they nullify the word of God (Matt. 15:3-6; 23:3, 23; cf. Mark 7:9-13). In contrast, Jesus *fulfills* the Torah by expounding upon its true meaning. He urges his followers to return "to the original intent of the Sinai instructions,"[16] a Torah observance guided by love and compassion.[17] He does not overthrow the Law; he explains it.[18] As David Sim writes, "This messi-

---

14 Ibid.
15 Ibid., 114.
16 Carmen Imes, *Bearing God's Name: Why Sinai Still Matters* (Downer's Grove, IL: Intervarsity Press, 2019), 142.
17 See J. Andrew Overman: "Matthew's community understands, teaches, and does the law. This is the fulfillment of the law and the righteousness which surpasses that of the Matthean antagonists. If you not only teach the law but do it, applying the dominant principles of love and compassion, you have fulfilled the law and properly enacted the will of God in heaven (7:12; 12:50; 21:31). Love and mutuality, as seen in the antitheses, guide the interpretation of the valid and enduring law" (*Matthew's Gospel and Formative Judaism: The Social World of the Matthean Community* [Minneapolis, MN: Fortress Press, 1990], 89).
18 See P. J. Hartin: "Matthew's Jesus does not take issue with the Torah as such, for the Torah is God's expressed will. Instead, Matthew's Jesus claims the role as official interpreter of God's will, of God's Torah" ("Ethics in the Letter of James, the Gospel of Matthew, and the Didache: Their Place in Early Christian Literature," in *Matthew, James, and Didache:*

anic exegesis goes beyond the letter of the law to reveal an even deeper meaning, and in doing so reveals God's true intentions in giving the Torah."[19]

As we examine each of Jesus's teachings in Matthew 5:21-48, we should recognize how they *affirm* rather than nullify the Torah. For instance, Jesus's prohibitions against anger (Matt. 5:21-26) and lustful looks (Matt. 5:27-30) get to the heart of the Torah's prohibitions against murder and adultery. By avoiding anger and lustful looks entirely, one will certainly fulfill the laws against murder and adultery. Thus, Jesus's teachings on anger and lustful looks explicitly uphold two of the Ten Commandments (Exod. 20:13-14).

Regarding Jesus's teaching on divorce (Matt. 5:31-32), it is probably the case that this saying is an extension of his prohibition against

---

*Three Related Documents in Their Jewish and Christian Settings* [Atlanta, GA: Society of Biblical Literature, 2008], 294). See also Hagner, 111: "By means of six bold antheses representing the teaching of Jesus, Matthew now contrasts Jesus' exposition of the true and ultimate meaning of the Torah with the more common, rabbinic understandings of the commandments. In this way the incomparable ethical demands of the kingdom are set forth, and in this way examples are provided showing how the righteousness of the Pharisees is to be exceeded."

19  David C. Sim, *The Gospel of Matthew and Christian Judaism: The History and Social Setting of the Matthean Community* (Edinburgh: T&T Clark Ltd, 1998), 130. See also W. D. Davies: "we cannot speak of the Law being annulled in the antitheses, but only of its being intensified in its demand, or reinterpreted in a higher key" (*The Setting of the Sermon on the Mount* [New York, NY: Cambridge University Press, 1963], 102). See also Lidija Novakovic: "Matthew portrays Jesus as the authoritative interpreter of the Torah whose halakhah reveals the will of God expressed in the Mosaic law" ("Matthew and Paul on Torah Observance: Is Matthew's Gospel Anti-Pauline, Pro-Pauline, or Un-Pauline?" in *To Recover What Has Been Lost: Essays on Eschatology, Intertextuality, and Reception History in Honor of Dale C. Allison Jr.*, ed. Tucker S. Ferda, Daniel Frayer-Griggs, Nathan C. Johnson [Boston, MA: Brill, 2021], 112).

lustful looks.[20] As Richard Averbeck explains, "the main point is to reinforce his teaching about not lusting after another woman."[21] Looking at a woman with lustful intent "could lead to a man wanting to divorce his wife for another woman, but, according to Jesus, sufficient grounds for divorce arises only if his wife commits some kind of 'unchastity.'"[22] From Jesus's perspective, if a man divorces his wife without legitimate grounds (even if he gives her a certificate of divorce), that divorce is invalid in God's eyes. Hence, marrying someone whose "divorce" is invalid is tantamount to committing adultery. Jesus's comments on divorce focus on preventing individuals from committing adultery, demonstrating yet another instance of Jesus *affirming* the Law.

What about Jesus's teaching to refrain from swearing oaths and instead speak the truth naturally (Matt. 5:33-37)? This prohibition aims to prevent individuals from violating the command against swearing falsely (Lev. 19:12). If one focuses on being truthful and dependable—letting his "yes" be yes and "no" be no—he will certainly fulfill the command against swearing falsely.[23] It should be noted that this saying concerns "relationships with other people in private life" and "does not forbid taking oaths in legal court cases, which the law sometimes required them to do in ancient Israel (see, e.g., Deut 6:13)."[24] Grant Osborne also provides some helpful remarks:

---

20   See Evans, 123: "It is in fact one antithesis, even though it is made up of two parts, the first treating the commandment not to commit adultery (vv. 27–30) and the second treating divorce law (vv. 31–32). They are tied together."

21   Richard E. Averbeck, *The Old Testament Law for the Life of the Church: Reading the Torah in Light of Christ* (Downers Grove, IL: IVP Academic, 2022), 237.

22   Ibid.

23   See Evans, 129: "Jesus' disciples are to be men and women of their word, not prevaricators and dissemblers, whose complicated and heavily qualified vows and oaths may in fact serve as camouflage for deceit."

24   Averbeck, 239.

[I]t is important to realize that Jesus is not revoking all oaths, for God makes oaths (Heb 7:20-22, 28) as does Paul (Rom 1:9; 2 Cor 1:23; Gal 1:20). Rather, frivolous oaths on ordinary issues, some of which might even support patent falsehood, are prohibited. The call is for honesty and integrity in every area of life.[25]

Regarding Jesus's teaching on retaliation (Matt. 5:38-42), we should recognize that the application of *lex talionis*, or the law of just compensation for loss ("eye for an eye," Exod. 21:23-25; Lev. 24:20; Deut. 19:21),[26] is intended specifically for judicial contexts, not for personal relationships in everyday life.[27] The purpose of this law was to "control excesses by saying that the payment should exactly fit the

---

25   Grant R. Osborne, *Matthew*, ECNT (Grand Rapids, MI: Zondervan, 2010), 204.
26   Except in the case of "life for life" (capital punishment for murder), *lex talionis* was not intended to be taken literally in the strictest sense. The Torah does not call for mutilation but rather compensation for loss. This is proven in Exodus 21:26-27, which immediately follows the "eye for an eye" passage in Exodus 21:23-25, where those who inflict bodily harm on a slave must set him free as compensation for the loss. See Paul Copan, *Is God a Vindictive Bully? Reconciling Portrayals of God in the Old Testament and New Testaments* (Grand Rapids, MI: Baker Academic, 2022), 71-86.
27   See W.D. Davies and Dale C. Allison: "Verses 38-42 are not a repudiation of Moses. While in the Pentateuch the lex talionis belongs to the judiciary process, this is not the sphere of application in Matthew. Jesus does not overthrow the principle of equivalent compensation on an institutional level—that question is just not addressed—but declares it illegitimate for his followers to apply it to their private disputes" (*Matthew: A Shorter Commentary* [New York, T&T Clark International, 2004], 82). See also Averbeck, 240: "It is most important to take note of the fact that [the law of just compensation for loss] always occurs in law court contexts, not personal relationships outside of court." See also Konradt, 86: "In the context of the Pentateuch's legislation, the *lex talionis* is not about establishing measures for taking justice into one's own hands, but about a principle for determining sentences in the courtroom."

crime and especially by making the punishment be part of the law court system rather than by individual vigilante actions."[28] However, it would seem that this law was being misapplied outside of court to justify personal vengeance (Matt. 5:39).[29] Such a misapplication of the law violates Leviticus 19:18 ("You shall not take vengeance"). In contrast, Jesus instructs his followers not to retaliate when wronged, but instead to be humble, generous, and to give more than what is asked of them. He is not contradicting the law but correcting its misapplication. Dale Allison puts it well:

> [W]hereas Matt. 5:38-42 concerns personal acts of vengeance by one wronged, Deuteronomy speaks to judges about how to administer the law. It is true that 5:40 refers to the court, but Jesus is not here delivering laws for the court to follow. He is rather speaking about interpersonal relations and declaring that it is illegitimate for his followers to apply the lex talionis to their private problems. So he is not overthrowing the principle of equivalent compensation on an institutional level.

---

28  Osborne, 208.
29  See Charles H. Talbert: "Apparently some who continued its strict usage took it as justification for personal acts of vengeance by the one wronged. Such an assumed interpretation seems necessary to make sense of the response by the Matthean Jesus: But I say to you, Do not retaliate against the evil person" (*Matthew*, PCNT [Grand Rapids, MI: Baker Academic, 2010], 86). See also Konradt, 86: "If we are to read the thesis in the sense of 5.20, as an example of how the Law was understood by the scribes and Pharisees, i.e., the understanding of the Law that underlies their inadequate level of justice, then what is criticized here is taking the *lex talionis* as a principle of behavior in personal conflicts, as though every individual has the right to respond to experienced injustice with 'appropriate' retaliation."

The subject of what is appropriate for the legal process is just not addressed.[30]

In his final antithetical saying, Jesus rejects the notion that we should hate our enemies and instead commands us to love them (Matt. 5:43-48). We should note that the Torah nowhere commands us to hate our enemy. As Averbeck writes, "Here it is important to remember that Jesus is not disputing the Law or the Prophets, but rather the way the scribes and Pharisees taught them in his day (Mt. 5:20)."[31] Indeed, Leviticus 19:18 explicitly commands us to love our neighbor. However, the scribes and Pharisees apparently interpreted this command in a narrow manner that excluded their enemies from the definition of "neighbor," giving themselves permission to hate their enemies. Such an approach abolishes the intent of the Law. As Wim Weren writes, "This more limited meaning of πλησίον ['neighbor'] contrasts sharply with Lev 19, where loving one's neighbor also includes loving the alien (compare Lev 19:18 with 19:34)."[32] In contrast to the scribes and Pharisees, Jesus fulfills the Law by giving the correct interpretation of it; he emphasizes that the command to love our neighbor includes our enemy (e.g., Exod. 23:4-5; Prov. 25:21). Weren continues: "Jesus chooses the same broadening approach that can be found in Lev 19. His listeners must not limit the concept of πλησίον ['neighbor'] to

---

30   Allison, 93.
31   Averbeck, 241.
32   Wim J. C. Weren, "The Ideal Community according to Matthew, James, and the Didache" in *Matthew, James, and Didache: Three Related Documents in Their Jewish and Christian Settings*, ed. Hubertus Waltherus Maria van de Sandt and Jürgen Zangenberg (Atlanta, GA: Society of Biblical Literature, 2008), 187.

those whom they love...but must also treat outsiders as their brothers and sisters, also if they are hostile to the community."[33]

As we have seen, none of Jesus's antithetical sayings in Matthew 5:21-48 nullify the Law of Moses. Again, such an understanding would contradict Matthew 5:17. Rather, it is the Pharisees' teachings that abolish the Law by undermining its authority. Jesus's teachings, on the other hand, *fulfill* the Law by drawing out its true meaning.[34]

## Conclusion

In Matthew 5:19, Jesus warns his followers not to disregard the Law of Moses and urges them to obey and teach it. While some have argued that the phrase "these commandments" in Matthew 5:19 refers to Jesus's own distinct commandments rather than those found in the Law of Moses, there is no textual support for this idea. The antitheses in Matthew 5:21-48 do not pit Jesus's teachings against the Torah but rather against the teachings of the religious leaders in his day. Hence, Matthew 5:19 is a direct teaching from Jesus to obey and teach even the least of the commandments found in the Law of Moses.

---

33  Ibid.
34  See Novakovic, 112: "the so-called antitheses...should be understood not as Jesus' attempts to abolish or bypass the law but as concrete examples of Torah observance that illustrate what the Matthean Jesus means by fulfilling the law."

CHAPTER 4

# BE BETTER THAN THE SCRIBES AND PHARISEES
## (MATTHEW 5:20)

In the previous two verses, Jesus taught that the Law of Moses will remain in force for as long as heaven and earth endure and admonished his followers to obey and teach it. Now, in Matthew 5:20, he demands that his followers surpass the righteousness of the scribes and Pharisees. In this chapter, we will discuss what this means.

## Surpassing the Righteousness of the Scribes and Pharisees

In Matthew 5:20, Jesus demands that his followers' righteousness exceed that of the scribes and Pharisees: "For I tell you, unless your righteousness exceeds that of the scribes and Pharisees, you will never enter the kingdom of heaven" (Matt. 5:20). What does Jesus mean by "righteousness"? In the context of Matthew's Gospel, this term denotes Torah observance,[1] hence Jesus speaks about "practicing" righteousness (e.g., Matt. 6:1).[2] This concept of righteousness comes

---

1   See Benno Przybylski: "the terms *dikaiosyne*, *dikaios* and *eleemosyne*, insofar as the latter is included in the doing of *dikaiosyne*, are used to describe the demand of God upon man to live according to a certain norm, the law." (*Righteousness in Matthew and his world of thought* [New York, NY: Cambridge University Press, 1980], 105).

2   See J. Andrew Overman: "Matthew explicitly speaks of 'doing righteousness' in 6:1, highlighting the praxis which is bound up with the term *dikaiosyne*" (*Matthew's Gospel and Formative Judaism: The Social World of the Matthean Community* [Minneapolis, MN: Fortress Press, 1990], 93).

from the Torah itself, which states that doing the commandments "will be righteousness for us" (Deut. 6:25).

In other words, Jesus expects his followers to obey the Law better than the scribes and Pharisees. By surpassing the scribes and Pharisees in their observance of the Torah, Jesus's followers exhibit a greater righteousness than them. Settling for an inferior righteousness on the level of the scribes and Pharisees results in exclusion from the kingdom entirely. As Steven Stiles writes:

> Jesus' teaching is the "fulfillment" and preservation of the Torah and Prophets (Matt 5:17-18), those who do and teach these commandments are great in the kingdom (Matt 5:19b), those who break these commandments are least in the kingdom (Matt 5:19a), and those who stoop to the standard of the scribes and Pharisees' righteousness will not even be allowed to enter (Matt 5:20, cf. 23:13).[3]

Thus, in agreement with the previous three verses, Matthew 5:20 further emphasizes Jesus's position that the Torah remains relevant and that his followers should obey it.[4] But how do Jesus's followers obey

---

3   Steven James Stiles, *Jesus' Fulfilment of the Torah and Prophets* (Tübingen: Mohr Siebeck, 2023), 89-90.
4   See Huub van de Sandt: "When Matthew has Jesus demand that the disciples' righteousness must exceed that of the scribes and Pharisees (5:20), he not only validates the continuance of the Torah (verse 18) but also the keeping of the 'least of these commandments' (verse 19)" ("Law and Ethics in Matthews' Antitheses and James's Letter: A Reorientation of Halakah in Line with the Jewish Two Ways 3:1-6," in *Matthew, James, and Didache: Three Related Documents in Their Jewish and Christian Settings*, ed. Hubertus Waltherus Maria van de Sandt and Jürgen Zangenberg [Atlanta, GA: Society of Biblical Literature, 2008], 330).

the Law *better* than the scribes and Pharisees? Here are three points to consider.

First, Jesus's followers must not disregard the commandments. While it is commonly assumed that Jesus mainly criticized the Pharisees for their "legalism" and excessive devotion to the Law, Scripture contradicts this assumption. In Matthew's Gospel, Jesus repeatedly accuses the Pharisees of hypocrisy and of neglecting important commandments (Matt. 15:3-6; 23:3, 23; cf. John 7:19). He never says that they are too focused on keeping God's commandments; on the contrary, he accuses them of "breaking" God's commandments (Matt. 15:3). Jesus's problem with the Pharisees is *not* that they are too devoted to the Law; rather, it is that *they lack sufficient devotion to the Law*. Indeed, the scribes and Pharisees "abolish" the Law through their false teachings and hypocrisy (cf. Matt. 5:17). This is why Jesus says that you cannot even be considered a genuine member of the kingdom if your righteousness is only as good as that of the scribes and Pharisees (Matt. 5:20). Hence, Jesus expects his followers to be *better* than the scribes and Pharisees—instead of disregarding and nullifying the commandments, we must obey and teach the commandments properly (Matt. 5:19).

Second, Jesus's followers must hold fast to God's word as our ultimate authority on matters of faith and practice. Throughout Matthew's gospel, Jesus criticizes the Pharisees not only for neglecting the commandments but also for emphasizing their traditions at the expense of the commandments. For instance, in Matthew 15:1-19, Jesus accuses the Pharisees of breaking God's commandments and nullifying God's word through their traditions. As J. Andrew Overman writes, "Jesus juxtaposes the Pharisees' traditions with the laws of God."[5] Hence,

---

5   J. Andrew Overman, *Church and Community in Crisis: The Gospel According to Matthew*

Jesus expects his followers to be better than the scribes and Pharisees in this regard—we must uphold God's word above man's traditions.

Third, Jesus's followers must follow his teachings. The biggest problem for the scribes and Pharisees is that many of them reject Jesus as the Messiah and as the authoritative interpreter of God's will. Therefore, they cannot fulfill the Law of Moses as God intended. In contrast, since Jesus gives the definitive interpretation of the Torah and lives it out fully, we must observe the Torah in accordance with his teachings and example. As Benno Przybylski writes, "Although the nature of the law never changes, the possibility of varying interpretations of the law is taken into account. Consequently, there are degrees of righteousness, the righteousness that exceeds that of the scribes and Pharisees being that which corresponds to the interpretation of the law given by Jesus."[6]

## Be Better Than the Pharisees—Really?

Does Jesus *really* expect his followers to exceed the righteousness of the scribes and Pharisees? Even though Jesus explicitly teaches that members of the kingdom must keep the Law better than the scribes and Pharisees, not everyone thinks that we should take this expectation from Jesus seriously. For instance, R. L. Solberg argues that it is "problematic" to understand Jesus's words "to mean that we need to keep the Law *even better than the Pharisees*."[7] Curiously, although Solberg outright dismisses this straightforward reading of the verse, he does not offer an alternative interpretation. Nevertheless, based on what he says next, I suspect that Solberg's objection stems from

---

(Valley Forge, PA: Trinity Press International, 1996), 225.
6   Przybylski, 105.
7   R. L. Solberg, *Torahism: Are Christians Required to Keep the Law of Moses?* 2nd ed. (Franklin, TN: Williamson College Press, 2022), 149. Emphasis in original.

what he perceives to be a contradiction between Matthew 5:20 and Paul's doctrine of justification by faith (e.g., Rom. 3:28). As Solberg goes on to argue, the notion that Jesus wanted his followers "to outdo the Pharisees in their study of, and dedication to, the Mosaic Law" is "based on an underlying, perhaps even subliminal belief that at least some level of effort is required on our part to truly achieve righteousness before God."[8] Hence, from Solberg's perspective, we cannot understand Matthew 5:20 to mean what it says because that would undermine the notion that we are justified by faith apart from works of the Law.

But is there really a conflict between Jesus's statement in Matthew 5:20 and Paul's doctrine of justification by faith? Not when we understand Matthew 5:20 within the "larger context of the verse (e.g., the grace of the beatitudes)," which "forbids us to conclude that entrance into the kingdom depends, in a cause-effect relationship, upon personal moral attainments."[9] In other words, Jesus's point is not that our righteousness "earns" us a place in the kingdom; his point is that members of the kingdom *will be* righteous.[10] Jesus expects those who have received the gift of God's kingdom to live in accordance with the demands of the kingdom. Those demands include obeying the commandments of the Torah.

Does Paul agree with Jesus that Christians should live righteously by obeying the Law of Moses? A straightforward reading of his letter to the Romans reveals that he indeed does. In fact, Paul's doctrine of

---

8   Ibid.
9   Donald A. Hagner, *Matthew*, WBC 33A (Dallas, TX: Word, 1993), 1:109.
10  See Ibid: "Entrance into the kingdom is God's gift; but to belong to the kingdom means to follow Jesus' teaching. Hence, the kingdom and the righteousness of the kingdom go together; they cannot be separated. And it follows that without this righteousness there can be no entrance into the kingdom (cf. 6:33)."

justification by faith *assumes* that those who have been declared righteous will live righteously. Two verses after he declares that believers are justified by faith apart from works of the Law, he immediately qualifies his statement so that he would not be misunderstood as saying that the Law is irrelevant. He explicitly states that those who are justified by faith will not overthrow the Law but rather uphold it (Rom. 3:31). Moreover, after announcing that believers are "under grace" and have been delivered from slavery to sin, Paul writes, "But thanks be to God, that you who were once slaves of sin have become obedient from the heart to the standard of teaching to which you were committed, and, having been set free from sin, have become slaves of righteousness" (Rom. 6:17-18). Hence, instead of submitting to "lawlessness leading to more lawlessness," Paul expects his readers to submit to "righteousness leading to sanctification" (Rom. 6:19). Finally, Paul teaches that the carnal mind opposes the Law and does not submit to it (Rom. 8:7), but the Holy Spirit enables believers to fulfill the Law's righteous requirements (Rom. 8:4). It is impossible to conclude from these statements that Paul thinks Christians should abandon the Law.

Additionally, in a passage very reminiscent of Matthew 5:17-20, Paul affirms the authority of "all Scripture" and emphasizes its usefulness in training believers "in righteousness" (2 Tim. 3:16). In context, Paul here is specifically referring to the Hebrew Scriptures or "Old Testament" (2 Tim. 3:15).[11] So, according to Paul, the Hebrew Scriptures are useful for training Christians how to live righteously. As Walter Kaiser writes, "One of the strongest statements on the authority and

---

[11] See Walter L. Liefeld: "The 'holy Scriptures' [mentioned in 2 Tim. 3:15] refer to what we know as the Old Testament and what the Jewish people call the Tanach" (*1 & 2 Timothy, Titus*, NIVAC [Grand Rapids, MI: Zondervan, 1999], 279).

use of the Old Testament Scriptures is found in 2 Timothy 3:15-16."[12] Thus, there is no disagreement between Jesus and Paul; both affirm that believers must live righteously in accordance with the Scriptures, including the Law of Moses.

## Conclusion

In Matthew 5:20, Jesus admonishes his followers to keep the Torah better than the scribes and Pharisees. We achieve this greater righteousness when we (1) obey and teach the Law instead of disregarding it, (2) prioritize God's word over human traditions, and (3) observe the Law in accordance with Jesus's interpretation. While some have proposed that a straightforward interpretation of Matthew 5:20 contradicts the doctrine of justification by faith, this idea is based on a misreading of both Jesus and Paul. In reality, both Jesus and Paul affirm that members of God's kingdom should live righteously by obeying the Torah.

---

12  Walter C. Kaiser, *The Promise-Plan of God: A Biblical Theology of the Old and New Testaments* (Grand Rapids: Zondervan, 2008), 354. See also Daniel I. Block: "this statement not only affirms the reliability of the Old Testament as divinely breathed Scripture, but especially that it is ethically relevant and through its application God creates a transformed people" (*The Gospel according to Moses: Theological and Ethical Reflections on the Book of Deuteronomy* [Eugene, OR: Cascade Books, 2012], 134).

# CONCLUSION

Sadly, many modern Christian teachers have adopted a stance on the Torah that is reminiscent of Marcion's. Like Marcion, these teachers insist that the Law of Moses and the Gospel of Jesus are incompatible and that Christians must unhitch from the Law entirely. However, as the previous chapters of this book have demonstrated, Jesus's words in Matthew 5:17-20 deter us from accepting this antinomian theology.

In Matthew 5:17, Jesus prohibits his listeners from even thinking that he came to abolish the Law and Prophets. Jesus announces that he did not come to nullify the Law and Prophets as a legal authority over the lives of his followers. Instead, he says that he came to fulfill the Law and Prophets—that is, he came to teach and demonstrate how to observe them properly.

In Matthew 5:18, Jesus states that nothing will pass from the Law until heaven and earth pass away and all is accomplished. In other words, according to Jesus, the whole Law will remain valid until the end of the present age. As long as heaven and earth exist, the Torah will remain binding.

On the basis of the Torah's ongoing validity, in Matthew 5:19, Jesus urges his followers to obey and teach even the least of the commandments. In other words, the Law remains valid not only in theory but also in practice. In fact, a believer's status in the kingdom is determined by whether or not he obeys and teaches the Law of Moses.

Finally, in Matthew 5:20, Jesus demands that his followers observe the Torah more fully than the scribes and Pharisees. This greater righteousness is accomplished by taking the Law seriously and adhering to Jesus's proper interpretation.

CONCLUSION

As we have seen, according to Matthew 5:17-20, the Law is not irrelevant. It is a foundational aspect of Christian discipleship.

## Theological Implications

The interpretation of Matthew 5:17-20 defended in this book raises questions about the relevance of certain commandments that are often neglected by Christians today. For instance, what should Christians do with the command to observe the Sabbath? Should Christians avoid eating unclean meats like pork and shellfish? The fact that Jesus affirms the ongoing validity of the whole Torah and admonishes his followers to keep even the least of the commandments should prompt us to consider these laws.

Regarding the Sabbath, I have written an entire book exploring this commandment in the Bible and early church history.[1] In my book, I show that the New Testament nowhere suggests that Jesus or the apostles abolished this commandment. The earliest Christians, including Gentiles, continued to keep the Sabbath throughout the New Testament. Indeed, even as late as the fifth century AD, most Christians outside of Alexandria and Rome were still keeping the Sabbath in addition to attending religious services on Sunday. Nevertheless, despite the New Testament's affirmations of this commandment, the majority of Christians in later centuries gradually abandoned the Sabbath. In light of Matthew 5:17-20, Christians ought to reconsider the significance of this commandment.

The same can be said for the commanded festivals of Leviticus 23 and the food laws of Leviticus 11. Throughout the New Testament, we see that the earliest Christians observed these commandments, and at

---

[1] David Wilber, *Remember the Sabbath: What the New Testament Says About Sabbath Observance for Christians* (Clover, SC: Pronomian Publishing, 2022).

## CONCLUSION

no point do the New Testament authors indicate that they have been repealed.[2] Again, Matthew 5:17-20 strongly affirms that Christians today should be keeping these commandments.

Apart from the Sabbath, festivals, and food laws, most modern Christians would affirm much of the Torah. For instance, most Christians agree that we should keep nine of the Ten Commandments, the laws regarding sexual ethics in Leviticus 18, and the laws about how we should treat our neighbor. That is because many of these laws are explicitly repeated in the New Testament. There are really only a few other commandments that modern Christians tend to overlook.[3] However, Jesus did say that disregarding even "the least of these commandments" impacts our status in the kingdom (Matt. 5:19). Christians do well, then, to study the Torah and think deeply about which commandments they can apply today. After all, Paul said that "all Scripture" is profitable for teaching righteous behavior (2 Tim. 3:16).

I hope that this study of Matthew 5:17-20 has blessed you. The Torah is a gift from God, and I pray that you will receive it and follow the commandments for God's glory as well as your own benefit.

---

[2] To learn more about the biblical festivals and their relevance to Christians, see David Wilber, *A Christian Guide to the Biblical Feasts* (St. Louis, MO: Independently Published, 2018). For an examination of the New Testament passages pertaining to the food laws, see David Wilber, "Should Christians Keep the Bible's Food Laws?" *David Wilber's Blog*, December 29, 2023; David Wilber, "Did Jesus Reject the Torah's Dietary Laws? (Mark 7:1-23)," *David Wilber's Blog*, July 24, 2022.

[3] One other example of a neglected commandment is the command to wear tassels on our garments as a reminder to observe the Law of Moses (Num. 15:37-41). The New Testament records that Jesus observed this commandment (Matt. 9:20). For more information on this commandment, see Tim Hegg, *Introduction to Torah Living* (Tacoma, WA: TorahResource, 2002), 167-168; J.K. McKee, *Torah in the Balance, Volumes I&II* (McKinney, TX: Messianic Apologetics, 2024), 570-581.

APPENDIX

# HAVE THINGS ALREADY PASSED FROM THE LAW?

As we saw in Chapter 2, Jesus declares that nothing will pass from the Law until heaven and earth pass away (Matt. 5:18). However, not everyone agrees that we should understand Jesus to have meant what he said in this verse. R. L. Solberg writes, "Jesus could not have meant there would be no change in the Law until heaven and earth pass away."[1] The reason that Solberg insists that Jesus "could not have meant" that nothing will pass from the Law until heaven and earth pass away is that he thinks "*some things have already passed from the law.*"[2] Solberg derives this conclusion from his interpretation of certain passages in Hebrews and Paul's epistles.[3]

As I mentioned in Chapter 2, drawing a conclusion about Matthew 5:18 from unrelated passages is not a sound interpretive approach. Instead, we should seek to understand this passage within its own context before consulting the broader canonical context.[4] Nevertheless,

---

1. R. L. Solberg, *Torahism: Are Christians Required to Keep the Law of Moses?* 2nd ed. (Franklin, TN: Williamson College Press, 2022), 143.
2. Ibid., 131. Emphasis in original.
3. Ibid., 131-143.
4. See Walter C. Kaiser: "*After* we have finished our exegetical work of establishing what, indeed, the author of the paragraph or text under consideration was trying to say, *then* we must go on to set this teaching in its total Biblical context by way of gathering together what God has continued to say on the topic. We should then compare this material with our findings concerning the passage being investigated. But mind this point well: canonical context must appear only as part of our summation and not as part of our exegesis" (*Toward an Exegetical Theology: Biblical Exegesis for Preaching and Teaching*

Matthew 5:18 is not the only verse in the Bible, and we should consider all Scripture as we build our theology. So, do Paul's epistles and the Book of Hebrews indicate that some commandments have already passed from the Law? I am not convinced they do.

In the following discussion, I will examine the passages that Solberg uses to argue that certain commandments have passed from the Torah and offer an alternative interpretation. As I will demonstrate, a pronomian reading makes better sense of the text in each case.

## Animal Sacrifices

Solberg mentions the Torah's instructions concerning animal sacrifices at the temple as his first example of something that "has passed from the Law." In support of this claim, Solberg quotes a verse from Hebrews, which says, "there is no longer any offering for sin" (Heb. 10:18). Based on this verse, Solberg argues that "the animal sacrifices commanded in the Torah are no longer required" because Jesus became the sin offering on behalf of believers.[5] Additionally, despite the Bible's detailed descriptions of animal sacrifices being performed during the future Messianic era (e.g., Ezek. 40-48),[6] Solberg insists, "To suggest that sin offerings will one day resume—as many of our Torah-observant friends do—is to propose the insufficiency of Christ's sacrifice on the cross."[7]

Does Solberg's interpretation of Hebrews 10:18 fit the context of Hebrews? Not according to New Testament scholars. As Matthew

---

[Grand Rapids, MI: Baker Book House, 1981], 83).

5   Solberg, 132-133.

6   For a study on how these future sacrifices do not conflict with the message of Hebrews, see Jerry M. Hullinger, "The Problem of Animal Sacrifices in Ezekiel 40-48," *Bibliotheca Sacra* 152 (July-September 1995), 279-289.

7   Solberg, 133.

Thiessen writes, "there simply is no evidence in Hebrews that the author rejects the ritual and cultic aspects of the Jewish law. Rather, there is strong evidence that he thinks these aspects of the law remain in effect at the time of his writing."[8] As an example, Thiessen highlights the author's lengthy explanation regarding how the Messiah can legitimately serve as a priest despite not being from the tribe of Levi. As Thiessen writes, "the author assumes that the law concerning the proper genealogical descent of Israel's priests—they must descend from the tribe of Levi—is still in effect."[9] Since the Messiah is from the tribe of Judah (Heb. 7:14), the Law of Moses prevents him from serving as a priest on earth: "Now if he were on earth, he would not be a priest at all, since there are priests who offer gifts according to the law" (Heb. 8:4).

But if the Torah prevents the Messiah from serving as a priest, then how can the author of Hebrews claim that the Messiah serves as our high priest and makes atonement for our sins? The author answers this question *not* by saying that the priestly and sacrificial laws have passed from the Torah. Again, his entire argument *assumes* that these laws remain in effect. Instead, he explains that the Messiah's priesthood functions in heaven, where his tribal lineage does not restrict him from serving as a priest: "For Christ has entered, not into holy places made with hands, which are copies of the true things, but into heaven itself, now to appear in the presence of God on our behalf" (Heb. 9:24). Thiessen puts this point well:

---

8   Matthew Thiessen, "Hebrews and the Jewish Law," in *So Great a Salvation: A Dialogue on the Atonement in Hebrews*, ed. Jon C. Laansma, George H. Guthrie, and Cynthia Long Westfall (New York, NY: T&T Clark, 2019), 185.

9   Ibid., 187.

> Jesus is not qualified to be a priest on earth precisely because the law has already established an earthly priesthood and, in stipulating a genealogically determined priesthood, precluded Jesus of the tribe of Judah from ever becoming a priest in the temple in Jerusalem. For the author, the law regarding priestly descent from Levi remains valid and permanently disqualifies Jesus from being a priest on earth. This fact confirms the author's argument that, if Jesus is a high priest, then he must be one in the celestial realm, a realm that does not require priests to be descendants of Levi.[10]

The fact that the author of Hebrews assumes the validity of these priestly and sacrificial laws undermines Solberg's claim that animal sacrifices have passed from the Law. Indeed, from the author of Hebrews' perspective, it seems that the entire sacrificial system will remain until the new heavens and new earth. The priesthood and animal sacrifices exist because humans are sinful and mortal, which are features of the present fallen age.[11] Once the present age comes to an end and the new heavens and new earth fully arrive, the earthly sacrificial system will indeed "vanish away" (Heb. 8:13).[12] However, the present age, symbol-

---

10  Ibid.

11  See Ibid., 192: "How can the immortal and perfect God dwell in the midst of sinful and mortal people? In the priestly worldview, the ritual purity system addresses the latter condition of people—their mortality—by prohibiting people who experience ritual impurities, which represent death or mortality…from entering into sacred space where God dwells. Consequently, according to priestly through, the wilderness tabernacle and later Jerusalem temple are shaped by and intended to function in a world governed by mortality."

12  See Jersper Svartvik: "The author states that he is living in the present time (9:9: *eis ton tairon ton enestekota*), but that he longs for 'the time of a better order' (9:10: *merchri kairou diorthoseos epikeimena*). The author argues that the invisible service—impossible

ized by the tabernacle, is "still standing" (Heb. 9:8-9). Hence, "there are priests who offer gifts according to the law" (Heb. 8:4). That is, according to the author of Hebrews, the earthly sacrificial system still serves a valid function and won't pass from the Torah until the present age passes away, which aligns with Matthew 5:18 perfectly.[13]

Beyond Hebrews, both the Gospel of Luke and the Book of Acts significantly challenge Solberg's claim that the Torah's instructions regarding animal sacrifices passed from the Law at the time of the Messiah's death and resurrection. At the end of his Gospel, immediately following Jesus's ascension, Luke describes the disciples as "continually in the temple blessing God" (Luke 24:53). Luke further presents the apostles as actively participating in the temple services long after Jesus completed his work on the cross (Acts 2:46; 3:1; 21:26).[14] In Acts 21,

---

to see for our human eyes and impossible to hear for our ears, and impossible to grasp for our minds—is already going on, in which Jesus Christ serves as the high priest. But the time of the new covenant has not been realized, not yet. It is in this context that the statement in Hebrews 8:13 should and must be read. Hence, the verse should not be interpreted as a prediction of the fall of the temple...but as an eschatological expectation, as a longing for the future, a yearning for a fulfilled and perfected world...When the new time comes, there is no need for a temple, because on that day there will be nothing but a heavenly service" ("Reading the Epistle to the Hebrews Without Presupposing Supersessionism," in *Christ Jesus and the Jewish People Today: New Explorations of Theological Interrelationships* [Grand Rapids, MI: Eerdmans, 2011], 86-87).

13  See Thiessen, 192-193: "Whatever the limitations of the earthly sanctuary and the laws pertaining to the sanctuary, priesthood, and cult, they are inexorably tied to the nature of this realm—since this realm is mortal all aspects of its cult have built-in limitations... The author of Hebrews believes that the time will come when the earthly cult will cease to exist, not because he has a negative view of the Levitical priesthood and earthly sanctuary, but because he believes that the mortal realm will disappear, obviating the need for the earthly cult and the laws that pertain to it. But, although Jesus the high priest has come, that time where mortality no longer exists has not yet arrived and so the two systems function concurrently."

14  See Michael P. Barber: "Acts 3 has Peter and John attend the temple at the very hour Jews

Paul goes to the extent of joining others in a Nazarite vow and participating in public worship at the temple to reassure the Jewish believers in Jerusalem that he did not teach against the Law (Acts 21:24).[15] Luke records that an offering was made for Paul and the others (Acts 21:26), which would have involved animal sacrifices, including a sin offering (Num. 6:14-17).[16]

The apostles' continued endorsement of the temple services and animal sacrifices long after Jesus completed his work on the cross contradicts what we would expect if the apostles believed such parts of the Law had passed away. Moreover, contrary to Solberg, the apostles certainly could not be said to have implied "the insufficiency of Christ's sacrifice" by observing these aspects of the Torah. The examples of the apostles' temple worship in Luke and Acts occur after Luke says that Jesus "opened their minds to understand the Scriptures" and explained to them how the Scriptures taught that he would suffer and rise from the dead, resulting in the forgiveness of sins (Luke 24:44-49). Thus, in the narrative of Luke and Acts, the apostles would have already understood the implications of Jesus's sacrifice. And yet, they continued to participate in the temple services, which undermines the notion that

---

gathered for the daily Talmid ritual (cf. Luke 1:9-10; cf. Acts 10:3, 30; Dan 9:3-19; Ezra 9:4-5; Jdth 9:1-14)" (*The Historical Jesus and the Temple: Memory, Methodology, and the Gospel of Matthew* [New York, NY: Cambridge University Press, 2023], 52.)

15   For a detailed exegesis of Acts 21:17-26 that concludes that Paul remained committed to Torah observance, see Gregory Scott McKenzie, "Pronomian Paradigm: A Pro-Torah, Christocentric Method of Theology and Apologetics" (Ph.D. diss., Liberty University, 2024), 35-171, https://digitalcommons.liberty.edu/doctoral/5623/.

16   See Barber, 52: "The precise meaning of the vow is a bit obscure, but more interpreters think it refers to the one sworn by Nazarites. In this case, the 'offering' in view would involve an animal sacrifice (Num 6:14, 16; m. Naz. 8-11). Regardless of what one makes of the specifics, Paul himself is depicted as participating in the temple cult."

participating in temple worship somehow diminishes the value of the Messiah's work.

But what about Hebrews 10:18? When we examine the context, it becomes apparent that the author is not addressing the Torah's animal sacrifice laws when he states that "there is no longer any offering for sin." Instead, he is discussing Jesus's one-for-all sacrifice, which he contrasts with the repeated animal sacrifices performed daily and yearly (Heb. 7:27; 9:12, 26; 10:10). Unlike the animal sacrifices, which could never take away sins (Heb. 10:4, 11), the author declares that the Messiah's sacrifice completely atones for sin in accordance with Jeremiah's New Covenant prophecy ("I will remember their sins and their lawless deeds no more"). Since the Messiah's once-for-all sacrifice sufficiently atones for sin, he does not need to offer himself again; hence, "there is no longer any offering for sin." Again, Hebrews 10:18 is speaking about *the Messiah's* offering for sin, not the Levitical animal sacrifices.[17] Thus, Solberg's assertion that animal sacrifices have already passed from the Law misinterprets Hebrews 10:18.

Additionally, since the author states that animal sacrifices could never take away sin (Heb. 10:4, 11), there is no conflict between the Messiah's once-for-all sacrifice and the apostles' continued endorsement of the Levitical animal sacrifices in the Book of Acts nor the Prophets' vision of sacrifices taking place in the future. Animal sacrifices could never detract from the sufficiency of the Messiah's sacrifice because they perform an entirely different function—they serve as a "shadow" that points to the reality accomplished by the Messiah (Heb. 8:5; 10:1)—and are thus complementary rather than contradictory. The analogy of baptism may help illustrate this point concerning

---

17  For more on this verse, see Tim Hegg, *A Commentary on the Book of Hebrews* (Tacoma, WA: TorahResource, 2016), 2.113-116.

the symbolic function of animal sacrifices. The ritual of baptism is a symbol of the salvation accomplished by the Messiah (Rom. 6:3-5). But nobody would argue that baptizing new believers detracts from the sufficiency of the Messiah. Only if someone believed that baptism had salvific power could it detract from the Messiah's work. However, there is no conflict when we understand that baptism (like animal sacrifices) is a "shadow" and not the reality itself. The Messiah's work and the ritual that points to his work are not mutually exclusive or opposed. Animal sacrifices could never take away sin—only the Messiah's sacrifice is sufficient for this purpose—but this does not mean that the Levitical sacrifices are invalid in their separate role of pointing toward the Messiah's work. As David Moffitt writes:

> [T]he author's arguments about the Law's limited powers of purification do not support the further inference that he rejects entirely sacrificial ritual and external purification, replacing or superseding them with something wholly other, something inimical to the Levitical rituals.[18]

Before we move on from the topic of animal sacrifices, the existence of these laws does raise the question: if these laws have *not* passed from the Torah, then why don't we observe them today? The answer is that the Torah requires animals to be sacrificed only at the temple in Jerusalem and under the supervision of the Levitical priests (Lev. 17:3-7; Deut. 16:1-2). The Law prohibits us from making animal sacrifices anywhere else. Since there is no temple or functioning Levitical

---

18  See David M. Moffitt, "Weak and Useless? Purity, the Mosaic Law, and Perfection in Hebrews," in *Law and Lawlessness in Early Judaism and Early Christianity*, ed. David Lincicum, Ruth Sheridan, and Charles Stang (Tübingen: Mohr Siebeck, 2019), 91.

Priesthood today, there is no way to obey these aspects of the Torah. When the Jewish people were in exile in Babylon, they were in a similar situation as we are today. Moses describes this exact scenario in Deuteronomy 30:1-3. Moses predicts that Israel would be scattered among the nations, which means that they would not be in the land and thus could not observe many of the Torah's commandments concerning the sacrificial system. Moses says that when they find themselves in this situation, they must return to the Lord and obey his commandments. In other words, even though Israel would be incapable of obeying many of the Torah's commandments while in exile, God still requires their heartfelt obedience to the commandments they *could* obey. The same thing is true for us. In our current situation, much of the Torah cannot be kept—not because those elements of the Torah have "passed from the Law" before Jesus said they would, but because our current situation prevents us from being able to observe them. Hence, we obey the commandments that we *can* obey. Again, as was the case when the Jewish people were exiled to Babylon, the fact that we cannot observe these laws is not evidence that they have passed away.

## Circumcision

As his second example, Solberg notes that Leviticus 12:3 commands parents to circumcise their sons on the eighth day of birth. Then, based on passages like 1 Corinthians 7:18 and Acts 15, Solberg declares, "The commands regarding circumcision have passed from the law."[19] However, Solberg's objection has significant problems. First, the passages he cites do not support this conclusion. Note that Leviticus 12:3, which reiterates the command given to Abraham and

---

19   Solberg, 136.

his offspring in Genesis 17:10-14,[20] emphasizes the duty of Israelite *parents* to circumcise their male infants on the eighth day of birth. This verse says nothing about whether adult Gentiles must get circumcised, yet the passages in the New Testament that Solberg cites are addressed to adult Gentiles. Since the Law of Moses does not give a general command for adult Gentiles to get circumcised, the apostles were not contradicting the Law by not requiring it of them.[21]

Additionally, as briefly mentioned earlier, Paul and James go to great lengths to demonstrate that they believe that the Torah, including the command for parents to circumcise their eight-day-old sons, remains valid. According to Acts 21:20-21, when Paul visited James in Jerusalem, James informed Paul that some Jewish believers heard a rumor that he taught against the Torah and discouraged Jewish believers from circumcising their sons. How did James and Paul respond to this rumor? *Was* Paul really teaching that Jewish believers should

---

20    Genesis 17:10-14 specifically states that the commandment of circumcision is given to Abraham and his offspring, starting with Isaac (Gen. 17:19). Furthermore, the command is to be carried out on the eighth day of birth (Gen. 17:12), as Isaac's example proves: "And Abraham circumcised his son Isaac when he was eight days old, as God had commanded him" (Gen. 21:4). The law in Genesis 17 does also require that Abraham's household circumcise their slaves, but there is no commandment in the text for adult Gentiles who might join the community to undergo circumcision.

21    One might point to Exodus 12:44-49 as counterevidence to the notion that the commandment of circumcision does not apply to adult Gentiles. However, this passage only prohibits uncircumcised adult Gentiles (and native Israelites; see Exod. 12:49 and Josh. 5) from eating the sacrificial meat of the Passover meal. If a Gentile wants to eat the Passover lamb, he must get circumcised. However, it is important to notice that this passage is not a *general* commandment for adult Gentiles to get circumcised. See McKenzie, 74: "what the Torah specifically requires for circumcision is not for *soteriological purposes* but for Gentiles who wanted to observe the rites of Passover... Legally speaking, biblical *adult* circumcision is for those who are foreigners who have joined themselves to Abraham and who want to walk in the *commandment of Passover*."

forsake the Law of Moses and should stop circumcising their sons? If he were, we would expect him to respond by saying, "These rumors are true. I teach that the Torah's expiration date was the arrival of Christ and that the commands regarding circumcision have passed from the Law." However, that is not what Paul did. Instead, Paul *refuted* the idea that he was against the Law of Moses. James instructed Paul to join others in a Nazarite vow and participate in worship at the temple (Acts 21:22-24), and Paul did exactly that (Acts 21:26). This was to reassure the believers in Jerusalem that the rumor about Paul was false: "Thus all will know that there is nothing in what they have been told about you, but that you yourself also live in observance of the law" (Acts 21:24). Why did the apostles want the people to think that Paul kept the Law of Moses and did not teach against it? Because Paul *did* keep the Law of Moses and did *not* teach against it.[22] This would include, as they specifically stated, the Torah's command to circumcise infant sons on the eighth day. Paul was not against the Law, and he was not against believers circumcising their sons as the Law requires.

We see this upholding of the Law of circumcision in Paul's own writings. In Romans, Paul proclaims that circumcision indeed has "value" (Rom. 2:25; 3:1-2). But if circumcision has "passed from the Law," then circumcision is a matter of indifference at best. So then, why does Paul say that it has value? It doesn't make sense for Paul to say

---

22  See McKenzie, 50: "The conclusion we must therefore come to is that since Paul is not a liar and that he is not a madman, the most logical and supported position is that Paul is telling the truth! This means that he is not preaching or writing about apostasy from Moses, but that he walks orderly, keeping the Law, just as James indicates. In order to concretely demonstrate Paul's doctrinal orthodoxy to all present in Jerusalem, he is directed by James to perform sacrificial and ceremonial laws, which are, in all likelihood, the Nazirite Vow of Numbers 6, in order to show this orderliness and his perseverance in the gospel approved by James, Peter, and John."

such a thing unless he really does believe that circumcision has value. Again, this statement from Paul contradicts what we would expect if Paul believed circumcision became irrelevant at the coming of the Messiah.

But what about the passages in the New Testament that seem to be against circumcision? Is there a way to reconcile them with the passages in which the apostles endorse circumcision? Again, when we understand what the Torah requires concerning circumcision, it is easy to see how the so-called "anti-circumcision" passages are not anti-circumcision or anti-Torah at all. In fact, as we will see, these same passages undermine Solberg's objection entirely.

So, what does the Law of Moses require regarding circumcision? As I mentioned earlier, the Torah *does not require* adult Gentiles to be circumcised. The command specifically calls for *parents* to circumcise their infant sons (Lev. 12:3). In fact, the Torah fully includes uncircumcised adult Gentiles in the faith community and expects them to obey all the commandments that apply to them, including things like the Sabbath, festivals, food laws, etc.[23] The only restriction placed upon uncircumcised adult Gentiles (and uncircumcised adult Israelites) is being able to eat the meat of the Passover sacrifice (Exod. 12:48). But uncircumcised adult Gentiles are still part of the faith community in every other context.[24] As we will see, by not mandating circumcision

---

23 In his Master's Thesis, Ben Frostad provides a helpful list of all the places where Gentiles ("strangers") are explicitly included in the Torah's legislation. For instance, the Torah expects Gentile followers of Israel's God to observe the Sabbath (Exod. 20:10; 23:12; Deut. 5:14), Unleavened Bread (Exod. 12:19), Shavuot (Deut. 16:11), Yom Kippur (Lev. 16:29), Sukkot (Deut. 16:14; Deut. 31:10-12), etc. For many more examples, see Ben Frostad, "He Made No Distinction: Gentiles and the Role of Torah in Acts 15" (Master's Thesis, Briercrest Seminary, 2021) 9-10.

24 Even though an uncircumcised Gentile (or Israelite) is prohibited from eating the

for adult Gentiles, the apostles were demonstrating that they were actually *more* faithful to the Torah's requirements compared to their opponents who were pushing for the adult Gentiles to get circumcised.

Now let's look at some of the passages that Solberg cites in support of his opinion that the New Testament contradicts the Law of Moses. The first passage Solberg cites comes from Paul's first letter to the Corinthian community:

> Was anyone at the time of his call already circumcised? Let him not seek to remove the marks of circumcision. Was anyone at the time of his call uncircumcised? Let him not seek circumcision. For neither circumcision counts for anything nor uncircumcision, but keeping the commandments of God.
> —1 Corinthians 7:18-19

---

Passover lamb, earlier in the chapter, he is still expected to observe other aspects of the festival, such as removing leaven from his dwelling, eating unleavened bread, and abstaining from leavened foods during the seven-day festival (Exod. 12:18-20). If either the uncircumcised Gentile or the native Israelite refuses to obey these laws, both are subject to the threat of being "cut off from the congregation of Israel" (Exod. 12:19). If an uncircumcised Gentile can be cut off from Israel, that means that, even though he is uncircumcised, he is still already included in the congregation of Israel. The Torah elsewhere commands these Gentile worshipers of Israel's God to keep the Sabbath and other festivals (Exod. 20:10; 23:10; Lev. 16:29; Deut. 16:11-14) and explicitly identifies them as covenant members of the community (Deut. 29:1, 10-14; Josh. 8:30-35). Presumably, uncircumcised adults could remain uncircumcised followers of Israel's God and never eat the Passover lamb, while still participating in every other aspect of Torah life. For more on Gentile Christian Torah observance, see Mark Nanos, "Paul's Non-Jews Do Not Become 'Jews,' But Do They Become 'Jewish'? Reading Romans 2:25-29 Within Judaism, Alongside Josephus," *JJMJS* 1 (2014), 26-53. For more on the significance of eighth-day circumcision, see Matthew Thiessen, *Contesting Conversion: Genealogy, Circumcision, and Identity in Ancient Judaism and Christianity* (New York, NY: Oxford University Press, 2011).

In this passage, Paul says that if someone came to faith in the Messiah already circumcised, he should not "remove the marks of circumcision." Here, Paul is speaking about a surgical method of foreskin restoration. During the Maccabean period, certain Jews went through this procedure as a means of renouncing their faith and assimilating into Greek culture (1 Macc. 1:15).[25] Obviously, the apostles opposed circumcised men reversing their circumcisions.

The next part of the verse is where the controversy lies: Paul tells uncircumcised men to "not seek circumcision." Is Paul contradicting the Torah here? Not at all. Remember, the commandment is for Israelite parents to circumcise their eight-day-old sons, yet 1 Corinthians 7:18 is addressed to adult Gentiles whom God has called into the faith. As we saw earlier, the Law of Moses does not require adult Gentiles to get circumcised to be part of the faith community, so Paul is not contradicting the Law by not requiring it of them.

Paul goes on to say, "for neither circumcision counts for anything nor uncircumcision, but keeping the commandments of God." This is a bizarre statement at face value considering that Paul elsewhere declares that circumcision has much value (Rom. 2:25; 3:1-2). So, how can he say here that circumcision does not count for anything? As scholars have suggested, Paul's statement appears to be hyperbolic.[26] He uses similar hyperbolic language elsewhere in 1 Corinthians. For example, in 1 Corinthians 3:5-7, he seemingly invalidates the ministry work of Apollos and himself: "So neither he who plants nor he who waters is anything, but only God who gives the growth" (1 Cor. 3:7). Paul is

---

25   Jason A. Staples, *Paul and the Resurrection of Israel: Jews, Former Gentiles, Israelites* (New York, NY: Cambridge University Press, 2024), 167n81.

26   Ryan D. Collman, "Just A Flesh Wound? Reassessing Paul's Supposed Indifference Toward Circumcision and Foreskin in 1 Cor 7:19, Gal 5:6, and 6:15, *JJMJS* 8 (2021), 40-42.

not saying that the work he and Apollos did was literally worthless. He is using hyperbolic language for the purpose of emphasizing the importance of God's work in the believer. Similarly, in 1 Corinthians 7:19, Paul is not saying that circumcision is literally worthless or irrelevant. He is using hyperbolic language to emphasize the importance of keeping God's commandments.

And this leads to the next point. Solberg would have you believe that Paul is disregarding the Law of Moses by not requiring adult Gentiles to circumcise. He cites 1 Corinthians 7:18 as evidence that Leviticus 12:3 has "passed from the Law." But if that were indeed the case, then Paul flatly contradicts himself in the next verse. Paul urges his readers, whether circumcised or uncircumcised, to keep "the commandments of God." The "commandments of God" include God's commandment in Leviticus 12:3 to circumcise your son on the eighth day.[27] This verse completely undermines Solberg's argument. Paul did not require adult Gentiles to get circumcised because the Law of Moses does not require it. But Paul *did* require all believers, whether circumcised or not, to keep the commandments of God. This implies that while Paul did not require adult Gentiles to get circumcised, he would have expected them to circumcise their sons on the eighth day in accordance with Leviticus 12:3. As Gregory Scott McKenzie writes:

> Unlike the babies of native-born Israel, *grown* Gentile converts are not *compelled* to circumcision. The command

---

[27] Some have attempted to reconcile this contradiction by proposing that Paul redefined "the commandments of God" to exclude the command of circumcision, but this suggestion seems contrived. Like other Jewish writers (Sir. 32:23-24; Matt. 19:17-19; Josephus, *Antiq.* 8.120), Paul usually employs the term "commandment" (ἐντολή) to refer to the Torah (Rom. 7:8-12; 13:9). See Ryan D. Collman, *The Apostle to the Foreskin: Circumcision in the Letters of Paul*, BZNW 259 (Berlin: de Gruyter, 2023), 43-44.

of circumcision is for *children* to be circumcised, not adults. However, it seems likely that, when Gentile converts have a child, they would circumcise their child on the 8th day in accordance with the Law, thus full societal integration would take place over time, through faith and faithful obedience.[28]

The second passage Solberg cites is Acts 15, the Jerusalem Council event. According to this passage, the apostles' opponents insisted that the Gentile believers must get circumcised to be considered "saved" and allowed to join the believing community (Acts 15:1, 5).[29] This was an unreasonable burden since, as we have already seen, the Law of Moses does not require adult Gentiles to get circumcised, especially not as a prerequisite to salvation and being received among God's people. Hence, when the apostles rejected this proposal and insisted that both Jews and Gentiles are saved by grace through faith in the Messiah and not through circumcision or Torah observance (Acts 15:11), they were *agreeing* with the Torah, not contradicting it. Just like ancient Israel was to receive uncircumcised "strangers" who professed faith in Israel's God, the apostles said that the Church must receive uncircumcised Gentiles who professed faith in Israel's Messiah.

---

[28] McKenzie, 98n257.

[29] During the Hasmonean period (140-37 BC), circumcision began to be associated with proselyte conversion—a ritual for turning Gentiles into Jews so they could be considered "saved" and fully included in the community. See Shaye J. D. Cohen, *The beginnings of Jewishness: Boundaries, Varieties, Uncertainties* (Los Angeles: University of California Press, 1999), 136-169. See also Benjamin John Stepan Szumskyj, "The Role of the Law in the Sanctification of the Believer Today: A Brief Introduction to Pronomianism" (Ph.D. diss., Liberty University, 2024), 123-125, https://digitalcommons.liberty.edu/doctoral/5479/.

Although the apostles, in agreement with the Torah, did not require adult Gentiles to get circumcised to join the community, they *did* expect them to observe the Torah's commandments as they walked out their faith. As William Willimon observes, "James seems to regard theses gentiles as analogous to 'strangers' in the Hebrew Scriptures."[30] Just as the strangers who joined Israel and worshiped their God were required to keep the commandments, so too are Gentiles who join the Christian community. Willimon continues, "Nowhere does Luke suggest that Jesus abrogates the Torah. Even gentiles are to keep that part of the Torah which applies to them as non-Jews."[31] Indeed, as we continue in Acts 15, we see that the apostles recognized the need for these Gentiles to be discipled and taught the Scriptures. So, the apostles proposed that the Gentile believers should initially adhere to four fundamental commandments derived from the Law of Moses (Acts 15:20).[32] These four commandments were intended as a starting point and served to demonstrate to the Jewish believers that the Gentile believers had fully committed to the God of Israel and his Torah. Additionally, James expected these Gentile believers to learn and begin obeying the rest of the commandments that applied to them as they attended synagogue services every Sabbath to hear the Law of Moses preached (Acts 15:21). This expectation is reminiscent of Deuteronomy 31:12, where both native Israelites and strangers are instructed to gather and hear the Law of Moses preached during the festival of Sukkot so that they may "be careful to do all the words of this law." Eyal Regev provides a good summary of Acts 15:20-21:

---

30  William H. Willimon, *Acts*, IBC (Atlanta, GA: John Knox Press, 1988), 130.
31  Ibid., 131.
32  Cf. Exod. 34:15; Lev. 17:13-16; 18; 20:6-21; Num. 25:1-2; Deut. 12:16, 23.

> The implications are that since the Torah is proclaimed and studied in the synagogue on a regular basis, the God-fearing Christians would gain further knowledge and adhere to Jewish law after being accepted into the (Jewish-) Christian community. The legal obligations of the Apostolic Decree may have been an invitation to observe Jewish law.[33]

So, as we see in Acts 15, it is true that the apostles did not require the circumcision of adult Gentiles as a prerequisite to salvation and inclusion among God's people. That is because the Law of Moses does not require such a thing. Solberg assumes that the apostles' *opponents* were rightly handling Scripture in Acts 15. In reality, the apostles' opponents were mishandling Scripture by trying to impose a requirement for fellowship upon the Gentiles that the Law of Moses does not mandate. The *apostles*, not their opponents, were the ones rightly handling the Scriptures. Acts 15 does not support the conclusion that the commands regarding circumcision have "passed from the Law," nor does it support the conclusion that the apostles disregarded the Torah. It actually proves the opposite. The apostles were applying the commands regarding circumcision correctly, and according to Acts 15:21, they expected all believers, Jew and Gentile alike, to continue learning and obeying the Torah.

Finally, Solberg also cites Galatians, where Paul seeks to dissuade his adult Gentile readers from getting circumcised.[34] However, Galatians does not support Solberg's conclusion that Leviticus 12:3 has

---

33   Eyal Regev, "The Gradual Conversion of Gentiles in Acts and Luke's Paradox of the Gentile Mission," in *Law and Narrative in the Bible and in Neighbouring Ancient Cultures*, ed. F. Avemarie and K. P. Adams (Tübingen: Mohr Siebeck, 2012), 361.
34   Solberg, 135.

passed from the Torah for the same reasons that have already been articulated above. Paul's Gentile readers in Galatians were persuaded by certain teachers that they must get circumcised to be considered full members of the faith community (Gal. 3:3), which is the same idea that the apostles' opponents were pushing in Acts 15.[35] Paul informs these Gentile believers that they are being misled. These Gentiles were looking to circumcision as the key to obtaining legitimate sonship and justification before God, and Paul informs them that this pursuit is a dead end. Circumcision cannot give that to them. After all, Ishmael got circumcised when he was thirteen, and yet did not inherit the promise despite his circumcision. Only being "in Messiah"—the son of Abraham *par excellence*—grants them the status of legitimate sonship (Galatians 3:26-29). Again, Paul's argument contradicts the Law of Moses only if we assume that the Law of Moses requires adult Gentiles to get circumcised to be considered members of the faith community. However, since we have established that the Law of Moses does not require this, there is no contradiction.

Additionally, in Galatians, Paul urges his readers to "fulfill the law of Christ" (Gal 6:2). Most scholars understand "law of Christ" to be a direct reference to the Law of Moses *as it is taught and exemplified by Christ*.[36] Todd Wilson explains that "to fulfill the law of Christ

---

35 See Todd A. Wilson: "the Galatians had become convinced that they needed circumcision in order to be saved. No doubt what was being touted in Antioch was also being promulgated in Galatia. Certain men were telling these believes, 'Unless you are circumcised according to the custom of Moses, you cannot be saved' (Acts 15:1). And evidently the Galatians were buying it" [*Galatians: Gospel-Rooted Living* [Wheaton, IL: Crossway, 2013], 92).

36 See references in David Wilber, "The Law of Moses vs. the Law of Christ (Galatians 6:2; 1 Corinthians 9:21)," *David Wilber's Blog*, Dec. 18, 2023.

would be to fulfill the law of Moses in a Christlike way."[37] Hence, Paul assumes the Torah's validity and application in Galatians, thereby implicitly affirming the command to circumcise one's sons on the eighth day. This contradicts what we would expect if Paul taught that Leviticus 12:3 had passed from the Law.

## The Priesthood

As his third example, Solberg cites the Torah's requirement that priests come from the tribe of Levi (Deut. 18:1-5). Then he writes, "Under the New Covenant, all that changed. Jesus was appointed our High Priest, despite being from the tribe of Judah."[38] Additionally, Solberg notes that the New Testament authors identify Christians in general as priests, even though the majority of Christians are not Levites either (e.g., 1 Pet 2:5, 9). Solberg insists that the New Testament authors would not teach such things "if they thought the priestly laws of Moses were still in effect."[39] Thus, according to Solberg, this is evidence that "the commands regarding the priesthood have passed."[40]

Do the passages in the book of Hebrews about the Messiah's heavenly priesthood suggest that the Levitical Priesthood has passed from the Law? Actually, the author of Hebrews draws the opposite conclusion. As I discussed earlier in this chapter, the author of Hebrews teaches that the Torah's requirements regarding priestly descent are still in effect. In Hebrews 8:4, the author claims that the Messiah does not serve as a priest on earth because the Torah has already appointed

---

37   Todd A. Wilson, "Law of Christ," *Dictionary of Paul and His Letters*, 2nd ed. (Downers Grove, IL: InterVarsity Press, 2023), 624.
38   Solberg, 136.
39   Ibid., 138.
40   Ibid., 139.

priests to serve on earth. That is why the Messiah's priesthood must be in heaven; it operates beyond the Torah's jurisdiction, which means the Torah cannot prevent the Messiah from serving as a priest, as it would if he were on earth.[41] Again, the author's entire argument for the legitimacy of the Messiah's priesthood *assumes* that the priestly laws remain valid.

But what about the fact that the New Testament authors identify Christians in general as priests? Does this prove that the Levitical Priesthood has been nullified? Once again, the apostles continued to recognize the legitimacy of the Levitical Priesthood long after the Messiah's death and resurrection (Luke 24:53; Acts 2:46; 3:1; 21:26). Unlike Solberg, the earliest Christians saw no conflict between the Levitical Priesthood and the priesthood of all believers. Why is that? Because the earliest Christians were familiar with the Torah. In Exodus 19:6, God calls *all* Israelites to be "priests" to the nations,[42]

---

41  See Moffitt, 101-102: "the author's comments about the Law's limitations with respect to perfection are not a dismissal of the legitimacy and authority of the Law within its proper sphere. In fact, in one of the more overlooked verses in modern Hebrews commentary the writer notes that the Law's authority prevents Jesus from being a priest on earth. Hebrews 8:4 reads that 'If he were on earth, he would not even be a priest because there exist those who offer the gifts in accordance with the Law.' The writer takes seriously the fact that Jesus has now passed through the heavens and entered God's presence. This is one of the reasons that Hebrews so consistently locates Jesus' priestly work in the heavens. On earth, the Law forbids him from legitimately holding priestly office and thus serving in priestly ministries (Heb 8:4). Such a claim indicates that the author has not simply dismissed the authority of the Law."

42  See Douglas K. Stuart: "Israel's assignment from God involved intermediation. They were not to be a people unto themselves, enjoying their special relationship with God and paying no attention to the rest of the world. Rather, they were to represent him to the rest of the world and attempt to bring the rest of the world to him. In other words, the challenge to be 'a kingdom of priests and a holy nation' represented the responsibility inherent in the original promise to Abraham in Gen 12:2–3: 'You will be a blessing. I will

even though he also calls only Levites to serve in the Levitical Priesthood. Significantly, the apostle Peter quotes Exodus 19:6 to support his claim that all believers serve as priests (1 Pet. 2:4-5). Both these "priesthoods" functioned concurrently in ancient Israel and during the time of the apostles.[43] Hence, the Levitical Priesthood and the priesthood of all believers are not mutually exclusive. The apostles referring to all Christians as "priests" does not invalidate the Levitical Priesthood any more than when God identified all Israelites as priests in Exodus 19:6.

## The Temple Veil

As his final example, Solberg cites the command to construct a veil in the tabernacle separating the Most Holy Place from the Holy Place (Exod. 26:31-35). Solberg then highlights the fact that when the Messiah died, the veil in the temple was torn in two (Matt. 27:50-51). Consequently, according to Solberg, this event "was Yahweh Himself bringing the old system of worship to an end."[44] However, Solberg's

---

bless those who bless you ... and all peoples on earth will be blessed through you.' Priests stand between God and humans to help bring the humans closer to God and to help dispense God's truth, justice, favor, discipline, and holiness to humans. Israel was called to such a function" (*Exodus*, NAC [Nashville, TN: B&H Publishing Group, 2006], 423).

43  It should be noted that the use of priestly imagery to describe believers who did not belong to the Levitical priesthood is not unique to Christian writers. The Qumran community described themselves as a spiritual temple and priesthood, and the Pharisees saw themselves as types of priests and their community as a spiritual temple. But neither of these Jewish groups imagined that they somehow replaced the Jerusalem temple or Levitical Priesthood. Even the Qumran community, which believed the Jerusalem priesthood was corrupt, still looked forward to proper temple worship in Jerusalem being restored in the future. For more on this, see Oscar Skarsaune, *In the Shadow of the Temple: Jewish Influences on Early Christianity* (Downers Grove, IL: IVP Academic, 2002), 112-121.

44  Solberg, 141.

conclusion reads too much into the text and seemingly contradicts the verses that come after. As Michael Barber writes, "Immediately following the tearing of the temple veil, Matthew goes on to call Jerusalem 'the holy city' (Matt 27:53). If Matthew's intention in narrating the torn veil is to highlight the Lord's departure from the temple, it would be excessively odd for him to go on a few verses later to define the city by its sanctity."[45] The tearing of the temple veil likely foreshadows the impending destruction of the Jerusalem temple in 70 AD as an act of God's judgment, but this does not imply that the New Testament authors regarded the temple and priesthood as no longer valid.[46] As discussed above, the apostles, even after the Messiah's resurrection and ascension, "were continually in the temple blessing God" (Luke 24:53; cf. Acts 2:46; 3:1; 21:26).

## Conclusion

In Matthew 5:18, Jesus states that nothing will pass from the Law until heaven and earth pass away and all is accomplished, which means nothing will pass from the Law until the end of the present world. Despite this straightforward reading of the text, Solberg has argued on the basis of certain passages from Hebrews and Paul's epistles that some commands—animal sacrifices, circumcision, the priesthood,

---

45  Barber, 73.
46  See Ibid., 110: "Jesus's prediction of the temple's end in the Gospel's overall narrative is not the result of a rejection of cultic worship. Judgment will befall Jerusalem first and foremost because of acts of wickedness committed by its leadership. The rejection of Jesus is part of this, and it is bound up with the failure of the leaders to recognize his messianic identity—the priests fail to grasp this in the temple (Matt 21:15) and the Pharisees do not recognize him as the figure from Psalm 118 who 'comes in the name of the Lord' (Matt 23:39). As in other works like Jeremiah and Daniel, the temple will not be spared in the coming cataclysm. Nevertheless, Jesus does not suggest that the sanctuary or its sacrifices are illegitimate. On the contrary, Jesus forcefully affirms their holiness."

etc.—have already passed from the Law. However, each of the passages cited in support of the claim that some commands have already been removed from the Law can be interpreted more convincingly *in alignment with* Matthew 5:18. The Book of Hebrews itself assumes the validity of the Levitical laws that pertain to the present age, which is "still standing" (Heb. 9:8-9). Moreover, the apostles' regular participation in the temple services confirms that they did not believe these commands had passed away. Regarding circumcision, since the Law of Moses does not require adult Gentiles to get circumcised, the apostles did not contradict the Law when they said that adult Gentiles did not need to be circumcised. Hence, the objections raised against a straightforward reading of Matthew 5:18 fail to convince. According to Jesus, as long as heaven and earth exist, the whole Torah will remain binding.

# POSTSCRIPT

There is so much more to discuss regarding the New Testament's teachings about the Law of Moses and whether Christians should keep it. This is one of my favorite topics, and I have many books, articles, and videos unpacking what the Bible says. I plan to continue studying and producing more content on this topic, and I want to invite you to join me on this journey.

How can you say connected? Here are several ways:

1. Sign up for my newsletter at www.davidwilber.com. You will receive an email notification whenever I release a new article or video.
2. Follow me on social media:
    Facebook: @DavidWilberBlog
    Instagram: @DavidWilberBlog
    Twitter: @DavidWilberBlog
    YouTube: @DavidWilberBlog
3. Reach out to me with questions or speaking invitations at www.davidwilber.com.

# BIBLIOGRAPHY

Allison, Dale C. *The Sermon on the Mount: Inspiring the Moral Imagination*. New York, NY: Crossroad, 1999.

Averbeck, Richard E. *The Old Testament Law for the Life of the Church: Reading the Torah in Light of Christ*. Downers Grove, IL: IVP Academic, 2022.

Banks, Robert. "Matthew's Understanding of the Law: Authenticity and Interpretation in Matthew 5:17-20." *JBL* 93, no. 2 (1974): 226-242.

Barber, Michael P. *The Historical Jesus and the Temple: Memory, Methodology, and the Gospel of Matthew*. New York, NY: Cambridge University Press, 2023.

Bauer, Walter. *A Greek-English Lexicon of the New Testament and Other Early Christian Literature*, rev. and ed. Frederick W. Danker, 4th ed. Chicago: University of Chicago Press, 2021.

Betz, Hans Dieter. *The Sermon on the Mount: A Commentary on the Sermon on the Mount, including the Sermon on the Plain (Matthew 5:3-7:27 and Luke 6:20-49)*. Hermeneia. Minneapolis, MN: Fortress Press, 1995.

Block, Daniel I. *The Gospel according to Moses: Theological and Ethical Reflections on the Book of Deuteronomy*. Eugene, OR: Cascade Books, 2012.

Charles, J. Daryl. "Garnishing with the 'Greater Righteousness': The Disciple's Relationship to the Law (Matthew 5:17-20)." *Bulletin for Biblical Research* 12, no. 1 (2002): 1-15.

Cohen, Shaye J. D. *The beginnings of Jewishness: Boundaries, Varieties, Uncertainties*. Los Angeles: University of California Press, 1999.

Collman, Ryan D. "Just A Flesh Wound? Reassessing Paul's Supposed Indifference Toward Circumcision and Foreskin in 1 Cor 7:19, Gal 5:6, and 6:15." *JJMJS* 8 (2021): 30-52.

———. *The Apostle to the Foreskin: Circumcision in the Letters of Paul.* BZNW 259. Berlin: de Gruyter, 2023.

Copan, Paul. *Is God a Vindictive Bully? Reconciling Portrayals of God in the Old Testament and New Testaments.* Grand Rapids, MI: Baker Academic, 2022.

Davies, W.D. *The Setting of the Sermon on the Mount.* New York, NY: Cambridge University Press, 1963.

Davies, W.D. and Dale C. Allison. *Matthew: A Shorter Commentary.* New York, T&T Clark International, 2004.

Duvall, J. Scott, and J. Daniel Hays. *Grasping God's Word: A Hands-On Approach to Reading, Interpreting, and Applying the Bible.* 3rd ed. Grand Rapids, MI: Zondervan, 2012.

Evans, Craig. *Matthew.* NCBC. New York, NY: Cambridge University Press, 2012.

Frostad, Benjamin. "He Made No Distinction: Gentiles and the Role of Torah in Acts 15." Master's Thesis, Briercrest Seminary, 2021.

González, Justo L. *The Story of Christianity, Vol. 1: The Early Church to the Dawn of the Reformation.* New York, NY: HaperCollins, 2010.

Hagner, Donald A. *Matthew 1-13.* WBC 33A. Dallas, TX: Word, 1993.

Hartin, P.J. "Ethics in the Letter of James, the Gospel of Matthew, and the Didache: Their Place in Early Christian Literature." Pages 289-314 in *Matthew, James, and Didache: Three Related Documents in Their Jewish and Christian Settings.* Edited by Hubertus Waltherus Maria van de Sandt and Jürgen Zangenberg. Atlanta, GA: Society of Biblical Literature, 2008.

Hegg, Tim. *A Commentary on the Book of Hebrews Chapters 9-13*. Tacoma, WA: TorahResource, 2016.

———. "An Investigation of 'The Lord's Table.'" Pages 93-112 in *Celebrate the Feast: Collected Articles on the Spring Festivals* (Tacoma, WA: TorahResource, 2019), 93-112.

———. *Introduction to Torah Living*. Tacoma, WA: TorahResource, 2002.

———. "What Does πληρῶσαι ('to fulfill') Mean in Matthew 5:17?" Paper presented at the ETS Annual Meeting, Nashville, TN, November 15-17, 2000. Accessed April 5, 2024. https://www.academia.edu/6582363/.

Hullinger, Jerry M. "The Problem of Animal Sacrifices in Ezekiel 40-48." *Bibliotheca Sacra* 152 (July-September 1995): 279-289.

Imes, Carmen. *Bearing God's Name: Why Sinai Still Matters*. Downer's Grove, IL: Intervarsity Press, 2019.

Kaiser, Walter C. *The Promise-Plan of God: A Biblical Theology of the Old and New Testaments*. Grand Rapids: Zondervan, 2008.

———. *Toward an Exegetical Theology: Biblical Exegesis for Preaching and Teaching*. Grand Rapids, MI: Baker Book House, 1981.

Keener, Craig. *The Gospel of Matthew: A Socio-Rhetorical Commentary*. Grand Rapids, MI: Eerdmans, 2009.

Kennedy, George A. *New Testament Interpretation Through Rhetorical Criticism*. Chapel Hill, NC: University of North Carolina Press, 1984.

Konradt, Matthias. *Christology, Torah, and Ethics in the Gospel of Matthew*. Translated by Wayne Coppins. Waco, TX: Baylor University Press, 2022.

Liefeld, Walter L. *1 & 2 Timothy, Titus*. NIVAC. Grand Rapids, MI: Zondervan, 1999.

MacArthur, John. *Ephesians*. The MacArthur New Testament Commentary. Chicago, IL: Moody Press, 1986.

McKee, J.K. *Torah in the Balance, Volumes I&II*. McKinney, TX: Messianic Apologetics, 2024.

McKenzie, Gregory Scott. "Pronomian Paradigm: A Pro-Torah, Christocentric Method of Theology and Apologetics." Ph.D. diss., Liberty University, 2024. https://digitalcommons.liberty.edu/doctoral/5623/.

Moffitt, David M. "Weak and Useless? Purity, the Mosaic Law, and Perfection in Hebrews." Pages 89-103 in *Law and Lawlessness in Early Judaism and Early Christianity*. Edited by David Lincicum, Ruth Sheridan, and Charles Stang. Tübingen: Mohr Siebeck, 2019.

Mohler, R. Albert. "Getting 'Unhitched' from the Old Testament? Andy Stanley Aims at Heresy." *Albert Mohler*. August 10, 2018. https://albertmohler.com/2018/08/10/getting-unhitched-old-testament-andy-stanley-aims-heresy/

Nanos, Mark. "Paul's Non-Jews Do Not Become 'Jews,' But Do They Become 'Jewish'? Reading Romans 2:25-29 Within Judaism, Alongside Josephus." *JJMJS* 1 (2014): 26-53.

Novakovic, Lidija. "Matthew and Paul on Torah Observance: Is Matthew's Gospel Anti-Pauline, Pro-Pauline, or Un-Pauline?" Pages 104-121 in *To Recover What Has Been Lost: Essays on Eschatology, Intertextuality, and Reception History in Honor of Dale C. Allison Jr*. Edited by Tucker S. Ferda, Daniel Frayer-Griggs, Nathan C. Johnson. Boston, MA: Brill, 2021.

Osborne, Grant R. *Matthew*. ECNT. Grand Rapids, MI: Zondervan, 2010.

Overman, J. Andrew. *Church and Community in Crisis: The Gospel According to Matthew.* Valley Forge, PA: Trinity Press International, 1996.

———. *Matthew's Gospel and Formative Judaism: The Social World of the Matthean Community.* Minneapolis, MN: Fortress Press, 1990.

Rabinowitz, Noel. "Yes, the Torah is Fulfilled, But What Does This Mean? An Exegetical Exposition." *Kesher: A Journal of Messianic Judaism* 11 (2000): 19-44.

Regev, Eyal. "The Gradual Conversion of Gentiles in Acts and Luke's Paradox of the Gentile Mission." Pages 349-371 in *Law and Narrative in the Bible and in Neighbouring Ancient Cultures.* Edited by F. Avemarie and K. P. Adams. Tübingen: Mohr Siebeck, 2012.

Sandt, Huub van de. "Law and Ethics in Matthews' Antitheses and James's Letter: A Reorientation of Halakah in Line with the Jewish Two Ways 3:1-6." Pages 315-338 in *Matthew, James, and Didache: Three Related Documents in Their Jewish and Christian Settings.* Edited by Hubertus Waltherus Maria van de Sandt and Jürgen Zangenberg. Atlanta, GA: Society of Biblical Literature, 2008.

Schweizer, Eduard. *The Good News according to Matthew.* London: SPCK, 1976.

Sim, David C. *The Gospel of Matthew and Christian Judaism: The History and Social Setting of the Matthean Community.* Edinburgh: T&T Clark Ltd, 1998.

Skarsaune, Oscar. *In the Shadow of the Temple: Jewish Influences on Early Christianity.* Downers Grove, IL: IVP Academic, 2002.

Snodgrass, Klyne R. *Ephesians.* NIVAC. Grand Rapids, MI: Zondervan, 1996.

———. "Matthew's Understanding of the Law." *Interpretation* 46 (1992): 368-378.

Solberg, R. L. *Torahism: Are Christians Required to Keep the Law of Moses?* 2nd ed. Franklin, TN: Williamson College Press, 2022.

Stanley, Andy. *Irresistible: Reclaiming the New that Jesus Unleashed for the World.* Grand Rapids, MI: Zondervan, 2018.

Stanton, Graham. *A Gospel for a New People: Studies in Matthew.* Edinburgh: T&T Clark, 1992.

Staples, Jason A. *Paul and the Resurrection of Israel: Jews, Former Gentiles, Israelites.* New York, NY: Cambridge University Press, 2024.

Stiles, Steven James. *Jesus' Fulfilment of the Torah and Prophets.* Tübingen: Mohr Siebeck, 2023.

Stuart, Douglas K. *Exodus.* NAC. Nashville, TN: B&H Publishing Group, 2006.

Svartvik, Jersper. "Reading the Epistle to the Hebrews Without Presupposing Supersessionism." Pages 77-91 in *Christ Jesus and the Jewish People Today: New Explorations of Theological Interrelationships.* Grand Rapids, MI: Eerdmans, 2011.

Szumskyj, Benjamin John Stepan. "The Role of the Law in the Sanctification of the Believer Today: A Brief Introduction to Pronomianism." Ph.D. diss., Liberty University, 2024. https://digitalcommons.liberty.edu/doctoral/5479/.

Talbert, Charles H. *Matthew.* PCNT. Grand Rapids, MI: Baker Academic, 2010.

Tertullian. *Adversus Marcionem.* Edited and translated by Ernest Evans. New York, NY: Cambridge University Press, 1972.

Thiessen, Matthew. "Abolishers of the Law in Early Judaism and Matthew 5, 17-20." *Biblica* 93, no. 4 (2012): 543-556.

———. *A Jewish Paul: The Messiah's Herald to the Gentiles.* Grand Rapids, MI: Baker Academic, 2023.

———. Contesting Conversion: Genealogy, Circumcision, and Identity in Ancient Judaism and Christianity. New York, NY: Oxford University Press, 2011.

———. "Hebrews and the Jewish Law." Pages 183-194 in *So Great a Salvation: A Dialogue on the Atonement in Hebrews*. Edited by Jon C. Laansma, George H. Guthrie, and Cynthia Long Westfall. New York, NY: T&T Clark, 2019.

Turner, David L. *Matthew*. BECNT. Grand Rapids, MI: Baker Academic, 2008.

Vines, Matthew. *God and the Gay Christian: The Biblical Case in Support of Same-Sex Relationships*. Convergent Books, 2014.

Weren, Wim J. C. "The Ideal Community according to Matthew, James, and the Didache." Pages 177-200 in *Matthew, James, and Didache: Three Related Documents in Their Jewish and Christian Settings*. Edited by Hubertus Waltherus Maria van de Sandt and Jürgen Zangenberg. Atlanta, GA: Society of Biblical Literature, 2008.

Wilber, David. *A Christian Guide to the Biblical Feasts*. St. Louis, MO: Independently Published, 2018.

———. "Did Jesus Reject the Torah's Dietary Laws? (Mark 7:1-23)," *David Wilber's Blog*, July 24, 2022. https://davidwilber.com/articles/did-jesus-reject-the-torahs-dietary-laws-mark.

———. *Remember the Sabbath: What the New Testament Says About Sabbath Observance for Christians*. Clover, SC: Pronomian Publishing, 2022.

———. "Should Christians Keep the Bible's Food Laws?" *David Wilber's Blog*. December 29, 2023. https://davidwilber.com/videos/should-christians-keep-the-bibles-food-laws.

———. "The Law of Moses vs. the Law of Christ (Galatians 6:2; 1 Corinthians 9:21)." *David Wilber's Blog*. December 18, 2023.

https://davidwilber.com/articles/the-law-of-moses-vs-the-law-of-christ.

Willimon, William H. *Acts*. IBC. Atlanta, GA: John Knox Press, 1988.

Wilson, Todd A. Galatians: Gospel-Rooted Living. Wheaton, IL: Crossway, 2013.

———. "Law of Christ." *Dictionary of Paul and His Letters*. 2nd ed. Edited by Scot McKnight, Lynn H. Cohick, and Nijay K. Gupta. Downers Grove, IL: InterVarsity Press, 2023.

Windsor, Lionel J. *Reading Ephesians and Colossians after Supersessionism: Christ's Mission Through Israel to the Nations*. Eugene, OR: Cascade Books, 2017.

www.ingramcontent.com/pod-product-compliance
Lightning Source LLC
Chambersburg PA
CBHW060344050426
42449CB00011B/2820